ARAB
IN
america

Toufic El Rassi

LAST GASP

Special Thanks to
Richard El Rassi
Lilian Jimenez
The School of the Art Institute of Chicago

Arab in America
Toufic El Rassi

Published by
Last Gasp of San Francisco
777 Florida Street
San Francisco, California, 94110
www.lastgasp.com

Ronald E. Turner, Publisher

Graphic Design
Lauren Emily McBlaine
Alex Laniosz

Production & Layout
Colin Turner

ISBN 978-0-86719-673-3

Third Printing, 2016
© 2007, 2016, Toufic El Rassi

Dedicated to my parents,
Aida & Metanios El Rassi

INTRODUCTION

A student of mine once proclaimed her desire to "fight to end racism." I thought about the possibility of a time when people don't allocate power and resources based on seemingly arbitrary markers of identity. I still think about that today.

My goal in making *Arab in America* was never so heady. I just remember people proclaiming the racial tolerance and magnanimity of American society and contrasting that sentiment with my life growing up in Chicago and its suburbs. Based on the reactions I have received since, many others have felt the vicious sting of prejudice because of their race, religion, or orientation while growing up in America. The book was meant as a rebuke and sort of catharsis for me. Ron Turner's support and belief in the project encouraged me further and I couldn't have asked for a more appropriate publisher in Last Gasp. In the years since, my attitude and beliefs have changed, but I am as opposed to the hypocrisy of the American political and cultural narrative as ever. We can believe in ideals, but do we believe them to soothe our otherwise disquieted consciousness? Or do we believe in ideals because they are worth fighting for and making real?

The United States elected Barack Obama since *Arab in America* was published. This historic event seemed improbable to me in 2008. In the aftermath of his election many proclaimed the eclipsing of racism in America. In the intervening years, race in this country has become more of a major issue in the headlines and discourse. This national concern with race is appropriate since the United States was built on a foundation of racism.

Trayvon Martin was killed, the uprisings of Ferguson and Baltimore were sparked by the killings of unarmed black men. Donald Trump's nomination was fueled (in part) by the hatred of Mexicans. Today the country seems riven by racial divides. These events have compelled America to more directly reckon with the ghosts of the past and present. I had another student once tell me that the racism directed towards black people is unique and distinct in its historical context compared to racism towards other non-whites. I agree with this; prejudice in America has its own idiosyncrasies and characteristics.

An interesting dimension of American racism is the fact that the amount of pigmentation of the skin is a central feature of classification. In recent years, American racial prejudice has mutated. It has become more nuanced, more complex and ignorant at the same time. The irony is quite hilarious. An Arab being called a dot-head is at once an expression of racism and cultural ignorance in one stroke. And yet I've had a young hijab-wearing woman protest to me that she experienced no racism growing up in a suburb of Chicago. I felt envious after I struggled with my scepticism.

The United States is getting browner. The resulting racial anxiety and nativist movement, reminiscent of the country's past, is sadly predictable. The fear of the other, the Muslim, the immigrant, of gay people, has been used by political and religious leaders since time immemorial toward the aim of achieving political power. This phenomenon repeats itself today. We blame ignorance, but is that enough? In other words, if people are taught that race is essentially a social construct, will we blunt or eliminate racism?

I don't know the answer to this question, but at the very least I believe in testimony. I also believe in exposure and speaking truth to power. I didn't like the prevailing narrative when it came to race in America, and I still don't. So I wrote a book. I am, however, encouraged by this generation of young people who are bravely confronting the status quo.

Toufic El Rassi

Chicago

2016

ARAB

IN
america

I REMEMBER SITTING THERE IN THE COMPUTER LAB AT SCHOOL

MY SISTER SENT ME AN EMAIL

Trinitron

@ Yahoomail

File Edit View Go Bookmark

YAHOO! MAIL   Welcome,

Date: 11 September 2001
From : ☺ "Linda"
Subject: Shave...
To : "Toufic"

Hey man you better shave...

IN THE HOURS AFTER THE ATTACKS A SPONTANEOUS DEMONSTRATION OF "PATRIOTISM" BROKE OUT IN BRIDGEVIEW IL, A SUBURB OF CHICAGO WITH A LARGE ARAB AND MUSLIM POPULATION

THE MOSTLY WHITE CROWD MARCHED TOWARD THE LOCAL MOSQUE, IT WAS UNCLEAR WHAT THEY WOULD DO IF THEY REACHED IT BECAUSE THE POLICE STOPPED THEM.

ONE OF THE MARCHERS TOLD THE PRESS:

I'M PROUD TO BE AN AMERICAN AND I HATE ARABS AND I ALWAYS HAVE.

IN AN ABC NEWS/WASHINGTON POST POLL 43% OF AMERICANS RESPONDED THAT THE ATTACKS MADE THEM "PERSONALLY MORE SUSPICIOUS" OF PEOPLE WHO APPEAR MIDDLE EASTERN.

THERE WERE ATTACKS AGAINST PEOPLE WHO WERE MISTAKEN FOR ARAB. A SIKH GAS STATION CLERK IN MESA ARIZONA WAS SHOT & KILLED. SIKHS WEAR TURBANS & HAVE LONG BEARDS.

FUCKING SAND NIGGERS!!

I HOPE WE NUKE THEM ALL TO HELL!

OH CRAP.

IT WAS A STRANGE, FAMILIAR SENSATION. I REMEMBER FEELING THE SAME WAY AFTER THE OKLAHOMA CITY BOMBING YEARS AGO...

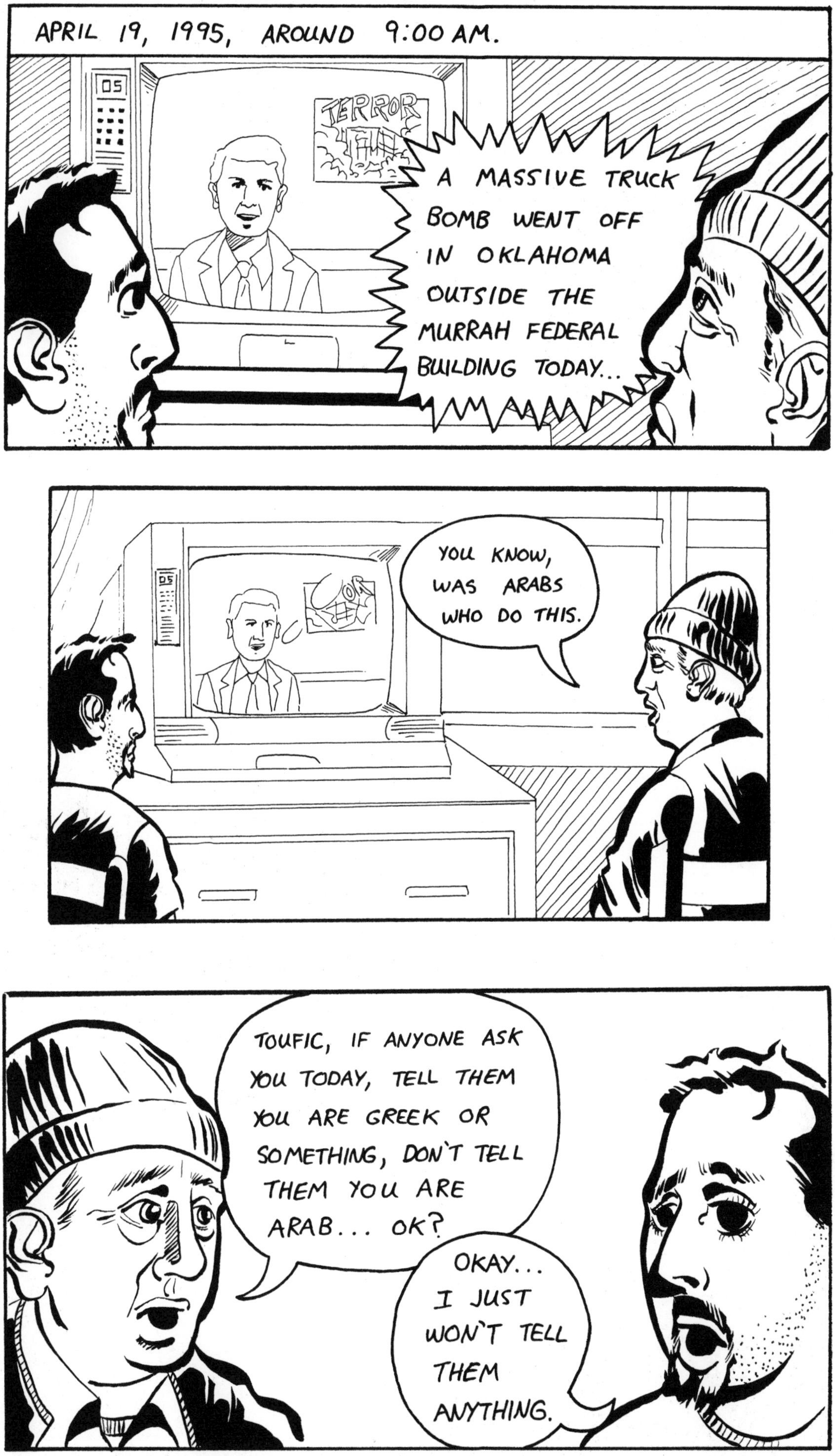
APRIL 19, 1995, AROUND 9:00 AM.
TERROR
A MASSIVE TRUCK BOMB WENT OFF IN OKLAHOMA OUTSIDE THE MURRAH FEDERAL BUILDING TODAY...
YOU KNOW, WAS ARABS WHO DO THIS.
TOUFIC, IF ANYONE ASK YOU TODAY, TELL THEM YOU ARE GREEK OR SOMETHING, DON'T TELL THEM YOU ARE ARAB... OK?
OKAY... I JUST WON'T TELL THEM ANYTHING.

BOMB WAS IN A RENTED
 AND IT WENT OFF
 PARENTS DROPPED
 KIDS OFF FOR DAY-
WE ALL WATCHED
 AFTERMATH ON T.V.
BODIES OF MEN, WOMEN,
CHILDREN WERE PULLED
 THE RUBBLE. 168
 DIED IN THE WORST
ORIST ATTACK ON U.S.
 UNTIL 9/11.

WHEN THE BOM.
HAPPENED, EVERYC
ASSUMED ARAB
TERRORISTS WER
RESPONSIBLE. IT
LATER DISCOVEREL
THE REAL CULPRIT
A CLEAN-CUT, WH
GULF WAR VETEF
FROM MIDDLE AM
NAMED TIMOTHY
MCVEIGH.

YOU KNOW BECAUSE THEY HATE ARABS.

YEAH BA, I ALREADY KNOW.

I KNEW WHAT MY DAD MEANT AND IT WAS NOT THE FIRST TIME I HAD THE DESIRE TO CONCEAL OR OBSCURE MY ETHNICITY, ESPECIALLY SINCE I WENT TO MOSTLY WHITE, MIDDLE OR UPPER CLASS SCHOOLS WHERE I TRIED DESPERATELY TO FIT IN AND BE ACCEPTED. IT WAS VERY DIFFICULT THOUGH BECAUSE I HAVE PRONOUNCED SEMITIC FEATURES COUPLED WITH DARK SKIN.

THERE EXISTS THE STEREOTYPE OF THE HIRSUTE ARAB WHICH HAS (LIKE MANY STEREOTYPES) A BASIS IN REALITY. I WAS IN 8TH GRADE WHEN MY BEARD GREW IN.

OBVIOUSLY THIS MADE ME A TARGET OF MUCH RIDICULE AMONG MY WHITE, ROSY-CHEEKED PEERS...

HEY! BEARDO!

HA HA HA HA!

I THINK THAT MOST NON-WHITE PEOPLE WHO GREW UP IN A MOSTLY WHITE ENVIRONMENT HAVE A STORY ABOUT THE FIRST TIME THEY REALIZED THAT THEY WERE NOT WHITE. I VIVIDLY REMEMBER THE FIRST TIME I DISCOVERED MY BROWN SKIN WHEN I WAS IN 8TH GRADE. GROWING UP, I NATURALLY ASSUMED EQUALITY OR (THANKS TO MY DOTING MOTHER) EVEN SUPERIORITY TO MY PEERS.

MY CLASS PERFORMED A VIDEOTAPED PRODUCTION OF "THE WIZARD OF OZ" FOR OUR SCHOOL PLAY. AND THE FOLLOWING DAY, WE WATCHED THE TAPE, DURING LUNCH. IMAGINE MY SHOCK UPON DISCOVERING THAT, IN SHARP CONTRAST TO THE ANGELIC WHITE FACES ARRAYED IN THE CHORUS, THE DARK SPLOTCH ON THE GRAINY TAPE WAS ME!

THAT WAS A VERY JARRING THING TO COME TO GRIPS WITH AS A BOY, AND IT WAS AT THAT MOMENT I REALIZED THAT I WAS DIFFERENT FROM OTHER KIDS. I FELT PANIC, I DIDN'T KNOW WHAT TO DO, I JUST WANTED TO LEAVE THE ROOM.

ONE DAY, WHEN I WAS ABOUT 13 YEARS OLD, I WAS OUT WITH MY MOTHER, SHE USUALLY PLAYED ARABIC MUSIC ON THE CASSETTE PLAYER IN THE CAR RADIO VERY LOUD WHICH ANNOYED ME.

WE DROVE THROUGH A PARKING LOT IN MY NEIGHBORHOOD AND TO MY UTTER MORTIFICATION, A CLASSMATE OF MINE CROSSED RIGHT IN FRONT OF US AS THE SPEAKERS BLARED THE WHINING VOICE OF UM KULTHUM.*

* UM KULTHUM IS ONE OF THE MOST POPULAR SINGERS IN THE ARAB WORLD.

I REACHED OVER AND SHUT IT OFF BEFORE MY CLASSMATE COULD SEE ME. LOOKING BACK, I DON'T KNOW WHY I WAS SO EMBARRASSED BUT AT THE TIME, I HATED THAT MUSIC.

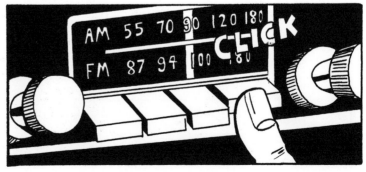

I AM NAMED AFTER MY GRANDFATHER, TOUFIC (PRONOUNCED TOO-FEEK OR TAU-FEEK) A RELATIVELY COMMON ARABIC NAME WHICH MEANS GOOD LUCK. LIKE MOST IMMIGRANTS, I HAD AN "AMERICAN" NAME. WHEN MY PARENTS FIRST ARRIVED TO THE UNITED STATES MY MOTHER CHANGED MY NAME TO DAVID BECAUSE THAT WAS THE ONLY NAME SHE KNEW THAT WAS WIDELY USED IN THE U.S. FOR YEARS I WAS KNOWN AS DAVID BUT AS I GOT OLDER I DECIDED TO GO BACK TO TOUFIC SINCE THAT WAS THE NAME ON ALL MY IDENTITY DOCUMENTS AND BESIDES I DON'T LOOK LIKE A DAVID ANYWAY SO IT'S NOT LIKE I WAS FOOLING ANYONE.

I'M ACTUALLY LUCKY BECAUSE WHEN MY YOUNGER SIBLINGS WERE BORN MY MOTHER WAS OBSESSED WITH GIVING THEM AMERICAN OR ENGLISH NAMES. SHE NAMED THEM AFTER PEOPLE SHE ADMIRED OR WHO WERE POPULAR AT THE TIME.

I HAVE A SISTER NAMED AFTER NANCY REAGAN.

AND ANOTHER NAMED AFTER THE LATE PRINCESS DIANA.

OKAY EVERYONE, LET'S GO AROUND THE ROOM & SHARE OUR NATIONALITY.

IT WAS THE FIRST DAY OF CLASS AT MY NEWEST SCHOOL WHEN MY NATIONALITY WAS REVEALED.

IRISH!

ITALIAN!

GERMAN AND ENGLISH.

I'M PART CHEROKEE!

POLISH!

I'M EGYPTIAN AND LEBANESE.

THE EGYPTIAN PART WAS OF PARTICULAR INTEREST TO MY CLASSMATES.

WALK LIKE AN EGYPTIAN!!

BOONGG! WALK LIKE AN EGYPTIAN

BANGLES

FOR SOME REASON, ARABS HAVE FIGURED PROMINENTLY IN SOME POP/ROCK SONGS. THIS WOULD BE YET ANOTHER CAUSE OF MUCH CONSTERNATION AND MISERY FOR ME AS A YOUNG MAN.

ALONG WITH "WALK LIKE AN EGYPTIAN" BY THE BANGLES, THERE WERE A FEW OTHERS...

THE CURE'S DEBUT ALBUM, "BOYS DON'T CRY" FEATURED THEIR HIT SINGLE "KILLING AN ARAB." EVEN THOUGH THE SONG WAS BASED ON "THE STRANGER," A NOVEL BY ALBERT CAMUS, I DON'T THINK THE KIDS HAD THAT IN MIND WHEN THEY USED IT TO MOCK ME.

AND I WOULD BE REMISS IF I FAILED TO MENTION THE SONG THAT STILL PLAYS SOFTLY IN THE BACKGROUND OF MY CHILDHOOD MEMORIES; PART OF THE "SOUNDTRACK OF MY CHILD-HOOD" IF YOU WILL. THAT SONG WOULD BE "ROCK THE CASBAH" BY THE INFLUENTIAL PUNK BAND "THE CLASH." THE SONG, COUPLED WITH THE VIDEO, HAUNTED ME AS A BOY- I STILL CRINGE WHEN I HEAR IT. I NEVER FIGURED OUT WHAT "SHARIF DON'T LIKE IT" MEANS, DON'T LIKE WHAT?

ALL THESE MEMORIES AND FEELINGS BUBBLED UP IN ME ON THE DAY OF THE ATTACKS. THIS ALMOST PAVLOVIAN RESPONSE REALLY SCARED ME. I FELT LIKE I SHOULD HIDE OR APOLOGIZE OR SOMETHING.

I DON'T KNOW WHY, BUT I FELT GUILTY, LIKE I DID SOMETHING WRONG AND SHOULD BE ASHAMED...

EVERYTIME I MADE EYE CONTACT WITH SOMEONE I QUICKLY LOOKED AWAY. I WAITED FOR SOMEONE TO WALK UP TO ME AND SAY "YOU! YOU ARE RESPONSIBLE FOR THIS!"

EVERYTIME I SAW A POLICE MAN I FELT AN ICY SHIVER DOWN MY BACK.

I BECAME EVEN MORE CONSCIENTIOUS ABOUT NOT DISPLAYING ANY SIGNS THAT COULD BE CONSTRUED AS SUSPICIOUS BEHAVIOR.

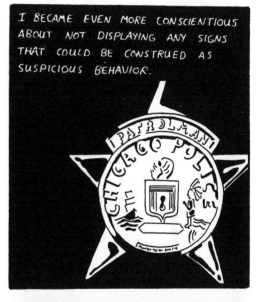

IF I KEPT LOOKING DOWN - THAT WAS TOO SUSPICIOUS, RIGHT?

OR IF I LOOKED AT HIM IN THE EYE THAT WOULD DRAW ATTENTION TO ME AND THAT'S BAD, RIGHT?

THERE WAS A GENERAL ATMOSPHERE OF SUSPICION AND FEAR. MANY ARABS AND MUSLIMS WERE DETAINED OR DEPORTED.

ANYONE WITH AN ARAB SOUNDING NAME COULD FEAR THE POSSIBILITY THAT THE FBI WOULD SHOW UP AT YOUR DOOR. ANYONE COULD JUST MAKE AN ANONYMOUS CALL TO THE FBI.

A NEIGHBOR CALLED THE FBI AND TOLD THEM THE ARAB MOTHER NEXT DOOR WAS RAISING A SUPPORTER OF HEZBOLLAH. THE FBI ACTUALLY INVESTIGATED THE 13 YEAR OLD BOY.

ON SEPTEMBER 12, 2002, A WOMAN IN A RESTAURANT IN GEORGIA CLAIMED THAT SHE OVERHEARD 3 "ARAB-LOOKING" MEN TALKING ABOUT A "TERRORIST PLOT."

IT TURNED OUT THEY WERE MEDICAL STUDENTS ON THEIR WAY TO SCHOOL IN FLORIDA. POLICE PULLED THEM OVER, SHUT DOWN THE HIGHWAY, HELD THEM AT GUNPOINT AND BLEW UP ONE OF THEIR BAGS WHICH HAD MEDICAL EQUIPMENT IN IT. ALL THIS HAPPENED AS NEWS HELICOPTERS COVERED IT LIVE ON TELEVISION.

TO THOSE WHO SCARE PEACE LOVING PEOPLE WITH PHANTOMS OF LOST LIBERTY, MY MESSAGE IS THIS: YOUR TACTICS ONLY AID THE TERRORISTS.

AFTER THE SEPTEMBER ATTACKS, THE U.S. GOVERNMENT QUESTIONED AND/OR DETAINED HUNDREDS OF ARABS AND MUSLIMS. THE EXACT NUMBERS ARE STILL UNKNOWN, BUT BY LATE NOVEMBER 2001, MORE THAN 1,200 PEOPLE HAD BEEN DETAINED AND HELD INCOMMUNICADO.

HADY HASSAN OMAR WAS HELD, WITHOUT CHARGE OR TRIAL, IN SOLITARY CONFINEMENT FOR 73 DAYS. HE MADE PLANE RESERVATIONS ON A COMPUTER AT A KINKO'S ABOUT THE SAME TIME ONE OF THE HIJACKERS DID SO AT THE SAME PLACE. AFTER REPEATED INTERROGATIONS AND HUMILIATING STRIP SEARCHES, HE WAS DECLARED INNOCENT AND RELEASED.

OSAMA ELFAR WORKED AT TRANS STATES AIRLINES IN ST. LOUIS AS A MECHANIC. HE WAS DETAINED IN SEPTEMBER 2001 AND HELD FOR 10 WEEKS BEFORE BEING DEPORTED TO EGYPT ON DECEMBER 4 AFTER BEING IN THE U.S. SINCE 1996. AFTER HIS DEPORTATION, ELFAR SAID:
"I THOUGHT EVERYONE HAS EQUAL RIGHTS NO MATTER THEIR SEX OR COLOR OR RELIGION... I DO NOT BELIEVE THAT ANYMORE."

ON SEPTEMBER 12 2006, I.C.E (IMMIGRATION AND CUSTOMS ENFORCEMENT) OFFICIALS SHOWED UP AT MY FAMILY'S HOUSE AT DAWN AND PULLED EVERYONE OUT OF BED. FORTUNATELY, I WAS NOT HOME AT THE TIME, BUT THE REST OF MY FAMILY WAS. THE WHOLE EXPERIENCE WAS QUITE JARRING AND INTIMIDATING.

AFTER ORDERING EVERYONE INTO THE LIVING ROOM, THEY BEGAN QUESTIONING THE WHOLE FAMILY.

THE WEIRD THING IS THAT THEY KNEW EVERYONE'S NAME AND SPECIFICALLY TARGETED THE MALES, ASKING THINGS LIKE:

ARE YOU A CITIZEN?

MY SISTER ASKED THE AGENTS WHAT THEY WANTED BUT THEY REFUSED TO ANSWER. THEY WENT TO EVERY ROOM, SEARCHING THE HOUSE.

CAN YOU TELL ME WHAT THIS IS ABOUT?

NO, SIT DOWN AND BE QUIET.

AFTER A WHILE, THEY PULLED OUT A PHOTO AND ASKED IF ANYONE RECOGNIZED THE MAN IN IT. THE MAN THEY WERE SEARCHING FOR WAS AN EX-BOYFRIEND OF MY AUNT WHO VISITED US SOME MONTHS EARLIER. IT TURNED OUT, HE HAD SOME KIND OF IMMIGRATION VIOLATION IN CANADA.

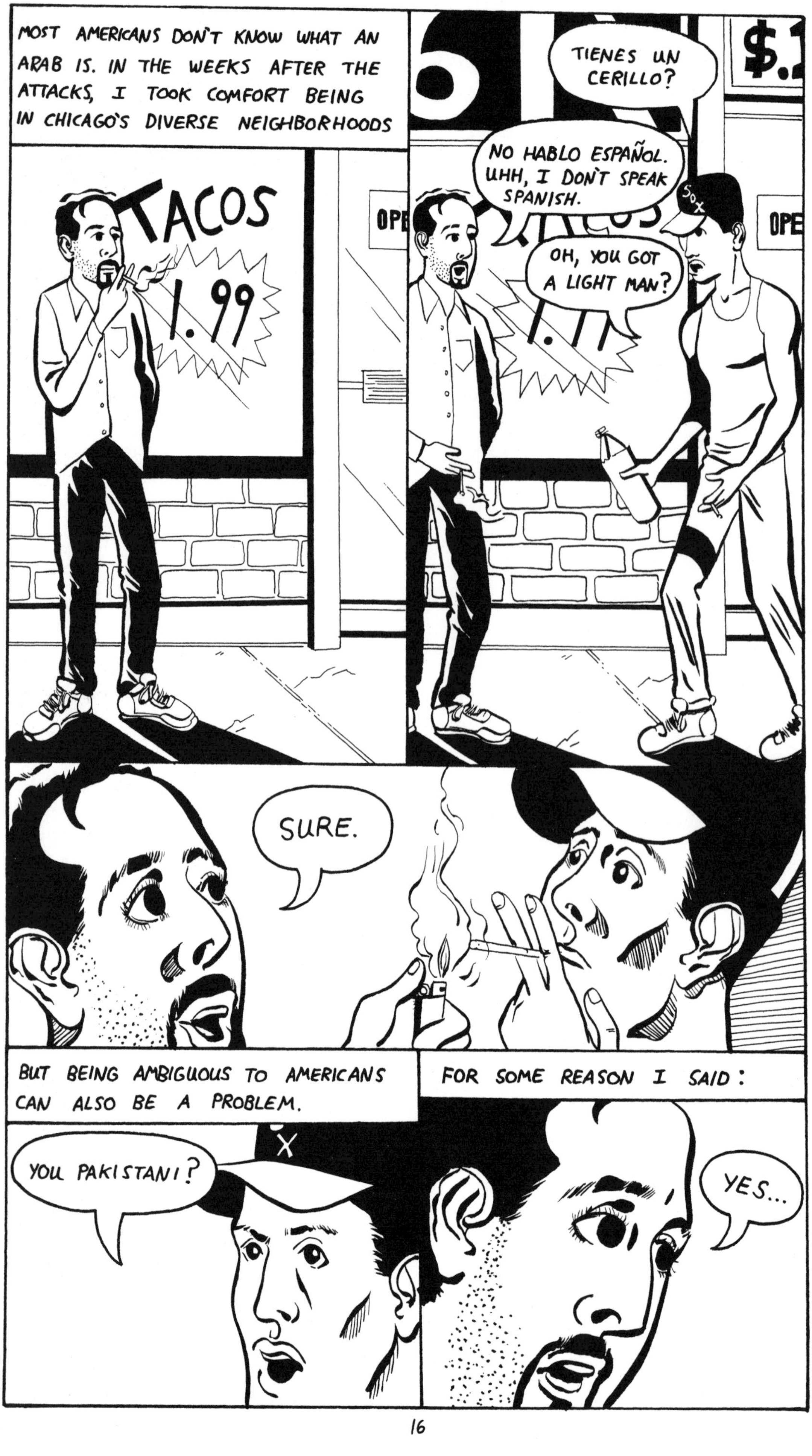
MOST AMERICANS DON'T KNOW WHAT AN ARAB IS. IN THE WEEKS AFTER THE ATTACKS, I TOOK COMFORT BEING IN CHICAGO'S DIVERSE NEIGHBORHOODS
TACOS
1.99
TIENES UN CERILLO?
NO HABLO ESPAÑOL. UHH, I DON'T SPEAK SPANISH.
OH, YOU GOT A LIGHT MAN?
SURE.
BUT BEING AMBIGUOUS TO AMERICANS CAN ALSO BE A PROBLEM.
FOR SOME REASON I SAID:
YOU PAKISTANI?
YES...

I IMMEDIATELY KNEW HE MEANT TO SAY PALESTINIAN SINCE THE 2 NATIONALITIES ARE OFTEN CONFUSED SINCE THEY SOUND SIMILAR.

SO YOU A TERRORIST MOTHER FUCKER?

WHAT? NO, NO, I'M NOT!

YES YOU ARE, I SAW YOUR FUCKIN' ASS ON TV.

JIMMY, TONY, THIS GUY IS A TERRORIST MOTHER FUCKER!

NO, NO, NO, DON'T DO THAT.

17

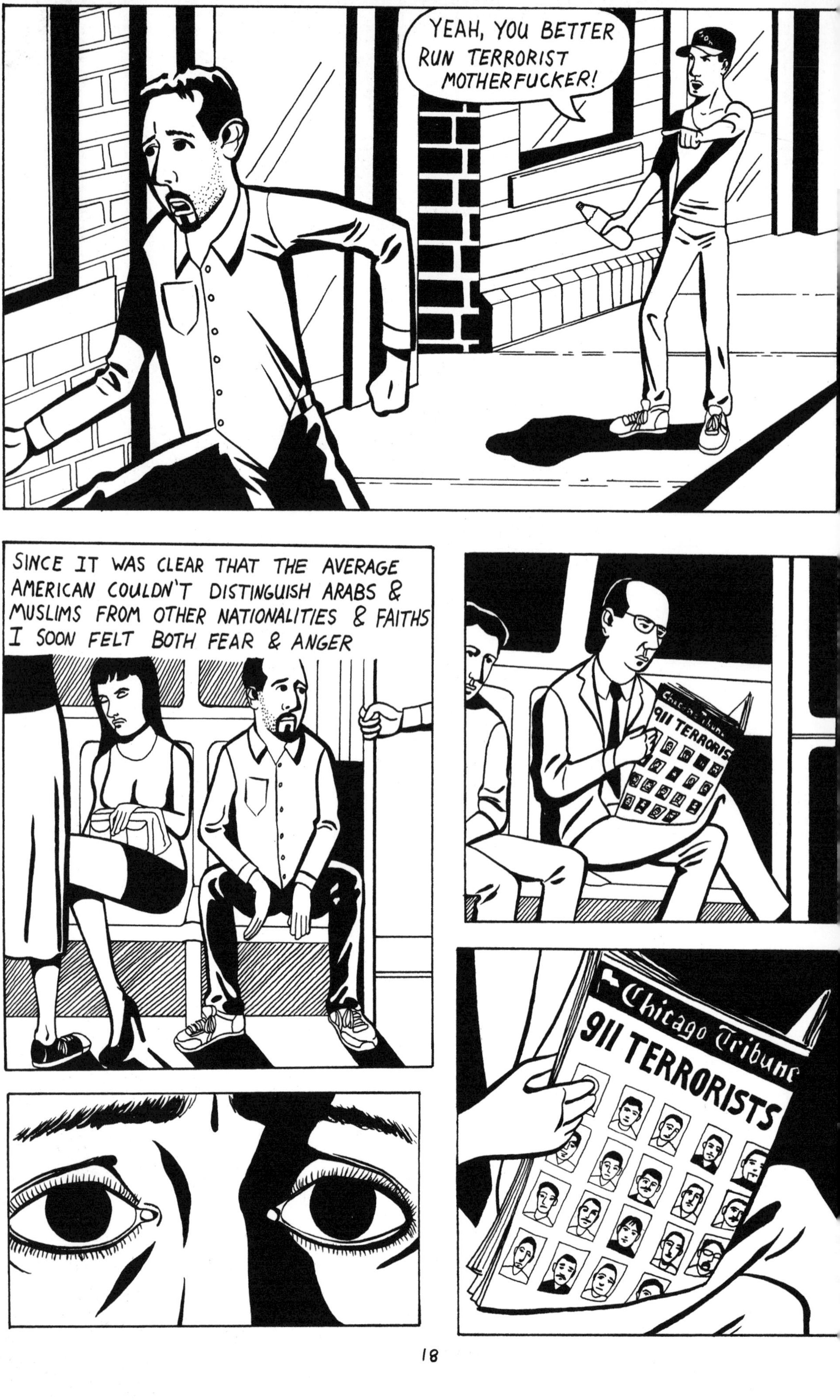
YEAH, YOU BETTER RUN TERRORIST MOTHERFUCKER!
SINCE IT WAS CLEAR THAT THE AVERAGE AMERICAN COULDN'T DISTINGUISH ARABS & MUSLIMS FROM OTHER NATIONALITIES & FAITHS I SOON FELT BOTH FEAR & ANGER
Chicago Tribune
911 TERRORISTS

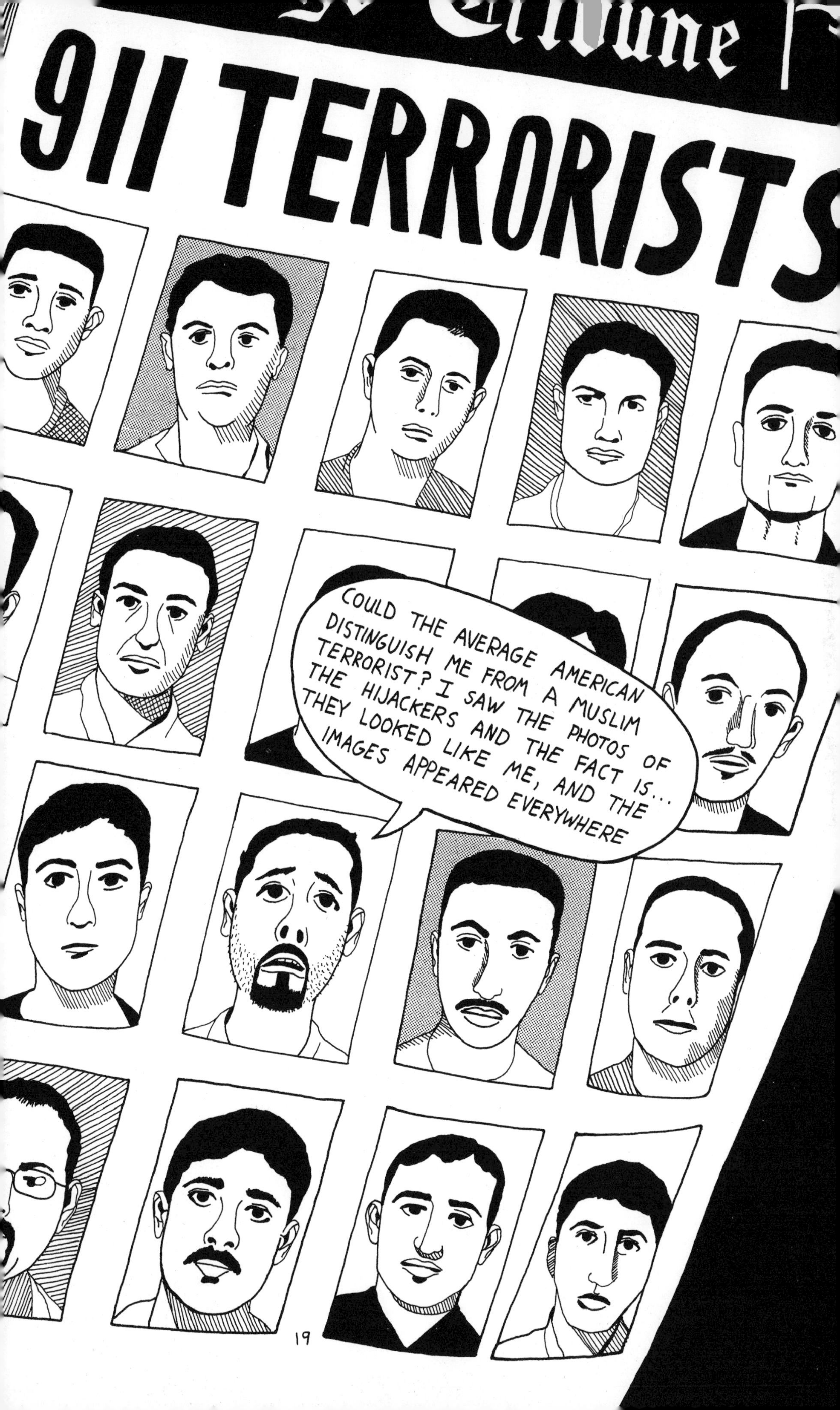

Tribune
911 TERRORISTS
COULD THE AVERAGE AMERICAN DISTINGUISH ME FROM A MUSLIM TERRORIST? I SAW THE PHOTOS OF THE HIJACKERS AND THE FACT IS... THEY LOOKED LIKE ME, AND THE IMAGES APPEARED EVERYWHERE

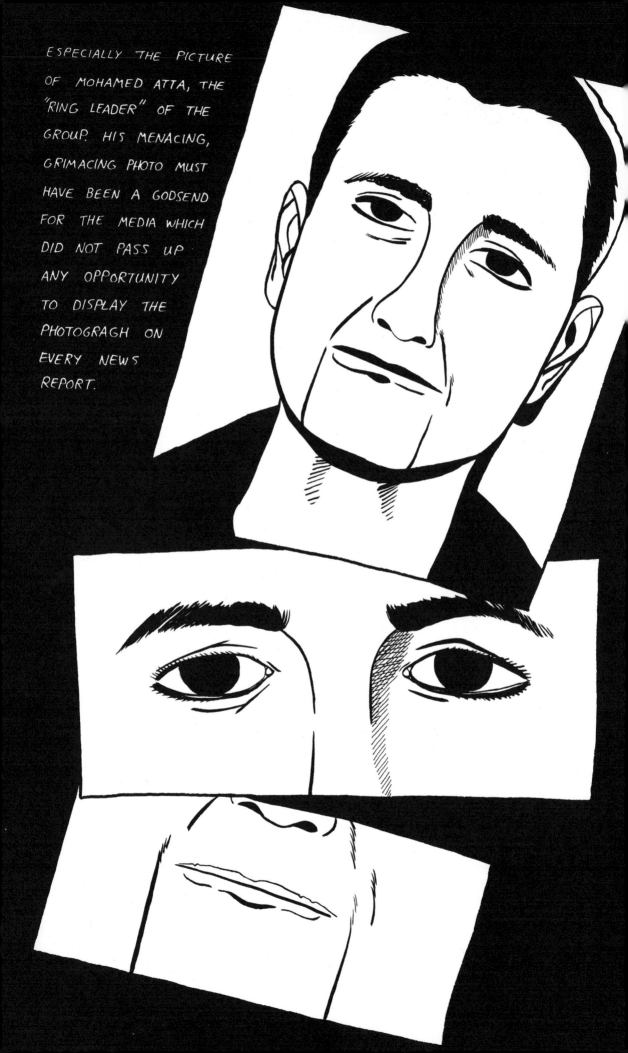

ESPECIALLY THE PICTURE
OF MOHAMED ATTA, THE
"RING LEADER" OF THE
GROUP. HIS MENACING,
GRIMACING PHOTO MUST
HAVE BEEN A GODSEND
FOR THE MEDIA WHICH
DID NOT PASS UP
ANY OPPORTUNITY
TO DISPLAY THE
PHOTOGRAGH ON
EVERY NEWS
REPORT.

ATTA'S PHOTO IS JUST ONE OF THE MANY EXAMPLES OF THE THREATENING PICTURES THE MEDIA USE. I SUPPOSE THAT IN ORDER FOR A SUSPECTED TERRORIST'S PHOTO TO GET MAJOR AIR PLAY IT HAS TO BE AS SCARY AS POSSIBLE, THAT'S PROBABLY WHY THE LESS FEARFUL PHOTOS OF ATTA'S COMRADES GOT LESS PLAY. NOTEABLE "MASTER MIND" PHOTOS INCLUDE: ABU MUSAB AL ZARQAWI, RAMZI BIN AL SHIBH, AND ABU ZUBAYDAH.

SOMETIMES THE PHOTOS THEY USE ARE QUITE EMBARRASSING AND INVITE MOCKERY. FOR EXAMPLE, WHEN YET ANOTHER "TERRORIST MASTERMIND," KHALED SHEIK MUHAMMAD, WAS ARRESTED IN PAKISTAN IN 2003, HE WAS IN BED ASLEEP. AS HE WAS TAKEN INTO CUSTODY, HE WAS DISORIENTED AND DISHEVELED AND STILL IN HIS PAJAMAS, WHEN SOMEONE TOOK A PHOTO THAT IS WIDELY USED IN THE PRESS.

THE BUSH ADMINISTRATION QUICKLY BLAMED USAMA BIN LADEN AND HIS AL QAEDA NETWORK FOR THE ATTACKS. BIN LADEN, A SCION OF A WEALTHY SAUDI ARABIAN FAMILY, WAS A LEADER IN THE FIGHT AGAINST THE SOVIET OCCUPATION OF AFGHANISTAN DURING THE 1980s. AFTER THE SOVIETS WERE DRIVEN OUT OF THE COUNTRY, BIN LADEN AND HIS COLLEAGUES TURNED THEIR ATTENTION TOWARD THE UNITED STATES.

AFGHANISTAN, A MUSLIM COUNTRY, SITUATED BETWEEN THE INDIAN SUBCONTINENT AND THE MIDDLE EAST HAS A LONG HISTORY OF CONFLICT AND COLONIAL DOMINATION. IN THE 19th CENTURY, THE RUSSIAN AND BRITISH EMPIRES COMPETED FOR CONTROL OVER THE COUNTRY AND EVENTUALLY, THE MODERN STATE OF AFGHANISTAN WAS CREATED IN 1919.

AFTER THE SOVIET WITHDRAWAL IN 1989, THE COUNTRY DESCENDED INTO CIVIL WAR UNTIL THE TALIBAN, A GROUP OF ISLAMIC STUDENTS, TOOK POWER IN 1996 AND CREATED A GOVERNMENT. THE U.S. AND ITS ALLIES INVADED ON OCTOBER 7, 2001 WHEN THE TALIBAN REGIME DID NOT IMMEDIATELY ACCEDE TO DEMANDS TO HAND OVER BIN LADEN WHO WAS HEADQUARTERED THERE.

THE TALIBAN, WHO ARE MOSTLY MADE UP OF THE PASHTUN ETHNIC MAJORITY, WERE OPPOSED BY AN ALLIANCE OF FACTIONS DRAWN MAINLY FROM AFGHANISTAN'S ETHNIC MINORITY TAJIKS, UZBECKS, AND HAZARAS, KNOWN AS THE NORTHERN ALLIANCE. THE TALIBAN HAD BEEN FIGHTING THEM FOR YEARS WHEN THE UNITED STATES INVADED. AFTER SIDING WITH THE NORTHERN ALLIANCE, THE U.S. WAS ABLE TO OUST THE TALIBAN REGIME IN LATE 2001.

THE TALIBAN WERE REPLACED BY A NEW REGIME HEADED BY PRO U.S. POLITICIAN HAMID KARZAI. AFTER A NATIONAL ASSEMBLY OR "LOYA JIRGA" IN 2002, KARZAI WAS CHOSEN TO ASSUME THE TITLE OF PRESIDENT AND IN 2004, AFGHANISTAN HELD U.S. BACKED ELECTIONS IN WHICH KARZAI WAS CONFIRMED AS THE NEW LEADER.

INFIGHTING BETWEEN LOCAL WARLORDS OVER POWER AND TERRITORY ERUPTED AFTER THE FALL OF THE TALIBAN. THE NEW LEADERS CONTINUE TO EXERT LITTLE CONTROL BEYOND THE CAPITAL AS VIOLENCE RACKS THE COUNTRY.

IN LATE 2003, NATO TOOK OVER THE U.N. INTERNATIONAL SECURITY ASSISTANCE FORCE (ISAF). IN 2005, NATO TROOPS EXPANDED INTO THE WESTERN AND CENTRAL PARTS OF THE COUNTRY BUT AS OF 2006 THE TALIBAN HAVE REEMERGED AS A POTENT MILITARY THREAT AND ARE WAGING A GROWING INSURGENCY AGAINST THE NATO FORCES IN THE SOUTH AND EAST.

IT IS SOMEWHAT IRONIC THAT THE U.S. HAS BECOME INVOLVED AGAIN IN AFGHANISTAN, SINCE IT ARMED AND FUNDED ISLAMIC MUJAHIDIN AFTER THE 1979 SOVIET INVASION. THROUGHOUT THE 1980s, BILLIONS OF DOLLARS AND MANY WEAPONS WERE FUNNELED THROUGH PAKISTAN TO FIGHT THE OCCUPATION.

EVEN THOUGH THE STRUGGLE AGAINST THE SOVIETS WAS A LEGITIMATE NATIONAL LIBERATION STRUGGLE THAT INCLUDED MANY DIFFERENT PARTIES AND GROUPS (INCLUDING WOMEN, MAOISTS, LIBERAL DEMOCRATS, ETC...), THE U.S. RECRUITED AND USED THE MOST RADICAL ISLAMISTS FROM THROUGHOUT THE MUSLIM WORLD TO FIGHT ITS PROXY WAR.

BESIDES BIN LADEN, GULBUDDIN HEKMATYAR IS A GOOD EXAMPLE OF THE KIND OF MEN ENLISTED AND FUNDED BY THE U.S. HIS FOLLOWERS WERE KNOWN FOR THROWING ACID INTO THE FACES OF WOMEN WHO DIDN'T WEAR A VEIL.

IF YOU ARE NOT WITH US – YOU ARE WITH THE TERRORISTS

BUT SUPPORT FOR THE WAR WASN'T UNIVERSAL.

AT MY COLLEGE, A STUDENT ANTI-WAR GROUP BEGAN HAVING PROTESTS AGAINST THE INVASION OF AFGHANISTAN.

OUR GRIEF IS NOT A CRY FOR WAR! THE U.S. HAS TO SERIOUSLY EXAMINE ITS FOREIGN POLICY AFTER THESE ATTACKS. WE HAVE TO ASK OURSELVES WHY SO MANY PEOPLE IN THE WORLD HATE US. AND IS ANOTHER WAR THE ANSWER?

HI TOUFIC, ARE YOU COMING TO OUR NEXT MEETING?

I HAD A CLASS ONCE WITH STACY AND SHE IGNORED ME THE WHOLE SEMESTER. NOW ALL OF THE SUDDEN SHE WAS FRIENDLY.

25

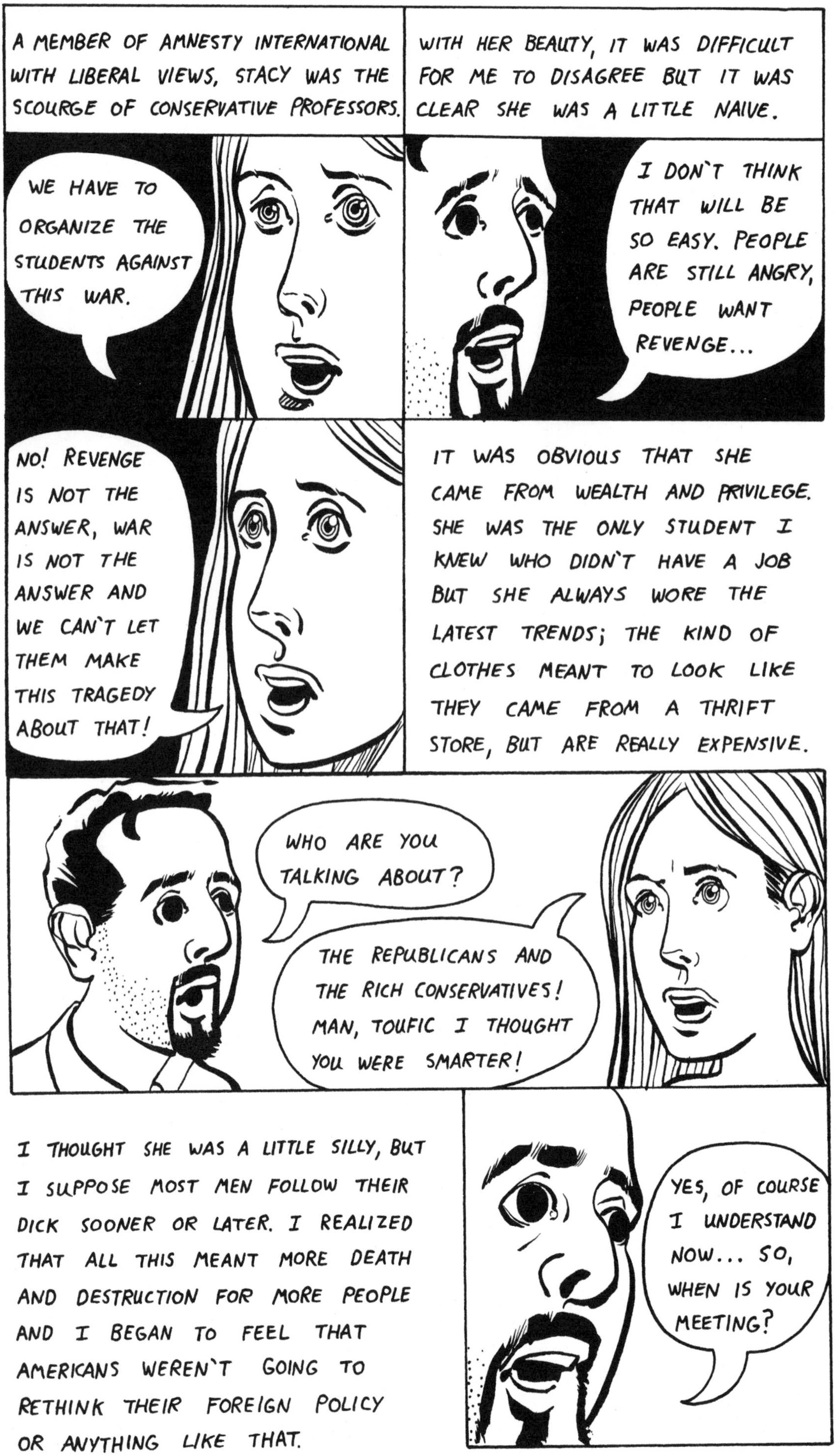
A MEMBER OF AMNESTY INTERNATIONAL WITH LIBERAL VIEWS, STACY WAS THE SCOURGE OF CONSERVATIVE PROFESSORS.
WITH HER BEAUTY, IT WAS DIFFICULT FOR ME TO DISAGREE BUT IT WAS CLEAR SHE WAS A LITTLE NAIVE.
WE HAVE TO ORGANIZE THE STUDENTS AGAINST THIS WAR.
I DON'T THINK THAT WILL BE SO EASY. PEOPLE ARE STILL ANGRY, PEOPLE WANT REVENGE...
NO! REVENGE IS NOT THE ANSWER, WAR IS NOT THE ANSWER AND WE CAN'T LET THEM MAKE THIS TRAGEDY ABOUT THAT!
IT WAS OBVIOUS THAT SHE CAME FROM WEALTH AND PRIVILEGE. SHE WAS THE ONLY STUDENT I KNEW WHO DIDN'T HAVE A JOB BUT SHE ALWAYS WORE THE LATEST TRENDS; THE KIND OF CLOTHES MEANT TO LOOK LIKE THEY CAME FROM A THRIFT STORE, BUT ARE REALLY EXPENSIVE.
WHO ARE YOU TALKING ABOUT?
THE REPUBLICANS AND THE RICH CONSERVATIVES! MAN, TOUFIC I THOUGHT YOU WERE SMARTER!
I THOUGHT SHE WAS A LITTLE SILLY, BUT I SUPPOSE MOST MEN FOLLOW THEIR DICK SOONER OR LATER. I REALIZED THAT ALL THIS MEANT MORE DEATH AND DESTRUCTION FOR MORE PEOPLE AND I BEGAN TO FEEL THAT AMERICANS WEREN'T GOING TO RETHINK THEIR FOREIGN POLICY OR ANYTHING LIKE THAT.
YES, OF COURSE I UNDERSTAND NOW... SO, WHEN IS YOUR MEETING?

IN FACT MANY OPINION MAKERS OPENLY CALLED FOR ALL OUT WAR ON THE ARAB/MUSLIM WORLD. CONSERVATIVE AUTHOR ANN COULTER MADE COMMENTS IN NATIONALLY SYNDICATED COLUMNS AND ON T.V. THAT WERE FANATICAL BUT STILL FOUND A RECEPTIVE AUDIENCE.

WE SHOULD INVADE THEIR COUNTRIES, KILL THEIR LEADERS AND CONVERT THEM TO CHRISTIANITY

CONGRESS COULD PASS A LAW TOMORROW REQUIRING THAT ALL ALIENS FROM ARABIC* COUNTRIES LEAVE... WE SHOULD REQUIRE PASSPORTS TO FLY DOMESTICALLY. PASSPORTS CAN BE FORGED, BUT THEY CAN ALSO BE CHECKED WITH THE HOME COUNTRY IN CASE OF ANY SUSPICIOUS SWARTHY LOOKING MALES

* I THINK SHE MEANT ARAB

JUST WHEN I THOUGHT THE HYSTERIA HAD REACHED ITS PEAK, ALAN DERSHOWITZ, A RESPECTED HARVARD LAW PROFESSOR ARGUED FOR THE LEGALIZATION OF TORTURE. AT ONE POINT HE SUGGESTS THE USE OF STERILIZED NEEDLES INSERTED BENEATH THE FINGERNAILS AS AN ACCEPTABLE METHOD.

THE REAL DEBATE IS WHETHER SUCH TORTURE SHOULD TAKE PLACE OUTSIDE OF OUR LEGAL SYSTEM OR WITHIN IT, THE ANSWER TO THIS SEEMS CLEAR: IF WE ARE TO HAVE TORTURE, IT SHOULD BE AUTHORIZED BY LAW.

I ORDINARILY WOULD HAVE DISMISSED THESE COMMENTATORS AND THEIR REMARKS AS THE RANTS OF A FEW OPPORTUNISTS WHO KNEW HOW TO GET AIR TIME. BUT AS REAL WORLD EVENTS SOON REVEALED, THESE SENTIMENTS HAD AN IMPACT ON NATIONAL POLICY. ILLINOIS REPRESENTATIVE MARK KIRK SOUNDED REASONABLE SAYING:

I'M OK WITH DISCRIMINATION AGAINST YOUNG ARAB MALES FROM TERRORIST-PRODUCING STATES. I'M OK WITH THAT... I THINK THAT WHEN WE LOOK AT THE THREAT THAT'S OUT THERE YOUNG MEN BETWEEN SAY, THE AGES OF 18 & 25 FROM A COUPLE OF COUNTRIES, I BELIEVE A CERTAIN AMOUNT OF INTENSE SCRUTINY SHOULD BE PLACED ON THEM... I'M NOT THREATENED BY PEOPLE FROM CHINA. I'M NOT EVEN THREATENED BY PEOPLE FROM MEXICO. I JUST KNOW WHERE THE THREAT IS FROM. IT'S FROM A UNIQUE PLACE, AND I THINK IT'S OK TO RECOGNIZE THAT.

IN 2002 WHITE HOUSE COUNSEL ALBERTO GONZALES WROTE A LEGAL MEMO TO PRESIDENT BUSH ARGUING THAT CAPTURED MEMBERS OF THE TALIBAN WERE NOT PROTECTED UNDER THE GENEVA POW CONVENTION.

THE NATURE OF [A WAR ON TERROR] PLACES A HIGH PREMIUM ON... FACTORS SUCH AS THE ABILITY TO QUICKLY OBTAIN INFORMATION FROM CAPTURED TERRORISTS AND THEIR SPONSORS AND THE NEED TO TRY TERRORISTS FOR WAR CRIMES... THIS NEW PARADIGM RENDERS OBSOLETE GENEVA'S STRICT LIMITATIONS ON QUESTIONING OF ENEMY PRISONERS.

[AND THAT] OUTRAGES UPON PERSONAL DIGNITY [AND] INHUMAN TREATMENT [ARE] UNDEFINED.

WAS THE WORLD GOING CRAZY? I GUESS I SHOULDN'T HAVE BEEN SO SURPRISED, AMERICANS TEND TO DISLIKE ARABS OR PEOPLE WHO ARE MISTAKEN FOR ARABS. IN FACT I THINK RACISM AGAINST ARABS IS ONE OF THE FEW PREJUDICES THAT IS NOT ONLY TOLERATED IN AMERICAN CULTURE BUT SOMETIMES ACTIVELY ENCOURAGED.

I REMEMBER IN HIGH SCHOOL, ONE OF MY MORE PATRIOTIC TEACHERS HAD A CARTOON PINNED TO THE WALL BEHIND HIS DESK.

WHEN THE FIRST GULF WAR BROKE OUT IN 1991, THERE WAS AN OUTPOURING OF ANTI-ARAB SENTIMENT. THIS MANIFESTED ITSELF ONCE IN MY HIGH SCHOOL SOCIAL STUDIES CLASS.

OKAY EVERYONE, AS YOU KNOW, THE WAR IN IRAQ JUST BEGAN SO I WANT ALL OF US TO KEEP OUR TROOPS IN OUR THOUGHTS AS THEY DEFEND OUR NATION.

YEAH!! WE'RE GOING TO SHOOT UP SOME TOWEL-HEADS!! U.S.A! U.S.A! U.S.A! U.S.A!!

HA HA HA U.S.A! U.S.A!

U.S.A U.S.A

HA! HA! HA! OKAY, OKAY, OKAY, NOW SETTLE DOWN NOW BOYS, HA! HA! HA! HA! BOYS!!

FOR ABOUT 43 DAYS AND NIGHTS THE U.S. AND ITS PARTNERS DROPPED 88,500 TONS OF BOMBS, THE EQUIVALENT OF SIX OF THE BOMB DROPPED ON HIROSHIMA DURING WWII. THIS WAS THE MOST SUSTAINED AND INTENSE BOMBING CAMPAIGN IN HISTORY.

IRAQ WAS DEVASTATED AND THE WAR WAS MOST CATASTROPHIC FOR THE CIVILIAN POPULATION SINCE THE BASIC INFRASTRUCTURE OF THE COUNTRY WAS TARGETED. BRIDGES, WATER TREATMENT PLANTS, ELECTRICAL PLANTS, ALL DESTROYED.

I DIDN'T APPRECIATE THE ENORMITY OF DESTRUCTION VISITED ON IRAQ UNTIL MUCH LATER. IN THE AFTERMATH OF THE WAR GEORGE BUSH DECLARED:

A NEW WORLD ORDER

THE MEDIA WAS LARGELY SILENT ABOUT ALL THIS - UNLESS YOU COUNT COMIC BILL HICKS WHO CAPTURED THE DISPROPORTIONATE NATURE OF THE WAR IN HIS ACT.

I GUESS THE MOST AMAZING THING ABOUT THE WAR, OBVIOUSLY THE DISPARITY IN THE CASUALTIES, IRAQ 150,000, U.S.A 79, HA HA

THE PATRIOTIC UPSURGE THAT CAME WITH THE WAR POPULARIZED THE SONG "PROUD TO BE AN AMERICAN," WHICH WAS PLAYED SO MUCH THAT EVEN I HAD IT MEMORIZED. I WENT TO A HIGH SCHOOL FOOTBALL GAME WHERE IT WAS PLAYED ALONG WITH THE NATIONAL ANTHEM.

ONCE THE SONG BEGAN EVERYONE IN THE AUDIENCE BEGAN TO SING TOGETHER IN A LOUD BOISTEROUS FASHION. I WAS SURROUNDED BY THESE PEOPLE SINGING A SONG THAT I ALSO KNEW BUT IT HAD NO CONNECTION TO ME WHATSOEVER. "PROUD TO BE AMERICAN?" ME?

IT'S LIKE WHEN PEOPLE SAY "OUR" TROOPS WHEN REFERRING TO THE U.S. MILITARY. AM I SUPPOSED TO SUPPORT "OUR" TROOPS? OR WHEN THEY SAY "WE" HAVE TO TAKE SADDAM OUT, OR "WE" HAVE TO GO TO WAR, WHO EXACTLY DO THEY MEAN BY "WE?"

32

I SHOULD MENTION THAT I DIDN'T ALWAYS FEEL THIS WAY; DURING THE 1980s, ACTION STAR SYLVESTER STALLONE MADE A SERIES OF VERY POPULAR FILMS THAT CAPTURED MY IMAGINATION. I WAS SUCH A BIG FAN OF RAMBO THAT THE WALLS OF MY ROOM WERE ADORNED BY THE MOVIE POSTERS.

AS A BOY, I REALLY WANTED TO "SERVE MY COUNTRY" AND BE A SOLDIER BUT THE GULF WAR CHANGED ALL THAT FOR ME. THE PROSPECT (IN FACT THE LIKELIHOOD) THAT I WOULD BE KILLING FELLOW ARABS ONE DAY JUST DID NOT APPEAL TO ME.

I ALWAYS WONDERED HOW GENERAL JOHN ABIZIAD WAS ABLE TO BE IN THE U.S. MILITARY. I MEAN HE IS A HIGHLY EDUCATED MAN WHO CAME FROM A LEBANESE FAMILY, WENT TO WEST POINT AND ROSE THROUGH THE RANKS TO BECOME A GENERAL. I WONDER HOW HE FELT WHEN HE COMMANDED FORCES IN IRAQ? I GUESS HIS NICKNAME, THE "MAD ARAB" MIGHT BE AN INDICATOR OF HIS ROLE IN THE U.S. MILITARY ESTABLISHMENT.

WHEN BAGHDAD FELL DURING THE 2003 WAR, I WAS IN A ROOM WITH SOME GRAD STUDENTS WATCHING IT LIVE ON T.V. I REMEMBER IT LIKE IT WAS YESTERDAY.

HA! WOULD YOU LOOK AT THAT!

WHOA! HA! WE'RE IN BAGHDAD BOYS!

CRAZY!

YOU SEE, TO THEM, THIS WAS AN AMAZING ACHIEVEMENT OF "OUR" TROOPS — A MOMENT OF PRIDE, REGARDLESS OF ONE'S STANCE ON THE WAR, A DEMONSTRATION OF "OUR" MILITARY MIGHT. A MOMENT OF VICTORY.

IT WAS UNCOMFORTABLE TO ME. ONE OF THE MOST IMPORTANT ARAB CAPITALS WAS BEING CONQUERED BEFORE MY EYES. HOW COULD I POSSIBLY FEEL PRIDE? I FELT THE OPPOSITE, SHAME, THAT A FOREIGN ARMY COULD SO EASILY CONQUER AND OCCUPY BAGHDAD.

34

BUT IT WAS DEFINITELY THE FIRST GULF WAR THAT SHAPED HOW I FELT ABOUT MY PLACE IN AMERICA. IT WAS SHOCKING TO DISCOVER THE LEVEL OF DEATH AND DESTRUCTION THE U.S. UNLEASHED ON AN ARAB COUNTRY. I EMPATHIZED MORE WITH THE IRAQIS THAN WITH THE HOOTING AND HOLLERING AMERICANS WHO CELEBRATED THE DESTRUCTION OF IRAQ IN THE POSTWAR PARADES. BUT THE WAR WAS JUST THE BEGINNING.

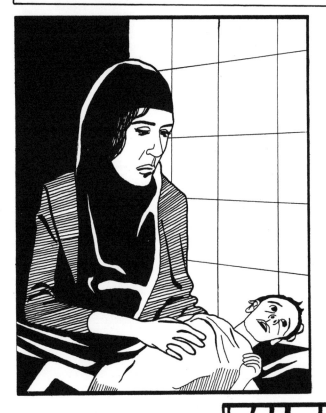

FOR MORE THAN 10 YEARS AFTER THE WAR THE U.S. HELPED MAINTAIN THE MOST STRINGENT ECONOMIC SANCTIONS AGAINST IRAQ. IMAGES OF SUFFERING IRAQIS MADE A LASTING IMPRESSION ON ME. SOME ESTIMATES SAY THAT AS MANY AS 500,000 IRAQI CHILDREN DIED FROM MALNUTRITION AND PREVENTABLE DISEASE AS A RESULT OF THE SANCTIONS.

WHEN ASKED BY A JOURNALIST ABOUT WHETHER THE SANCTIONS WERE WORTH THE DEATHS, THEN SECRETARY OF STATE MADELEINE ALBRIGHT REPLIED:

IT'S A DIFFICULT CHOICE BUT YES THE PRICE IS WORTH IT...

WAS IT OKAY THAT IRAQIS SUFFERED BECAUSE THEY WERE ARABS?

THE AMOUNT OF SUFFERING IN IRAQ IS UNCONSCIONABLE AND BESIDES IT ONLY MAKES HUSSEIN STRONGER SINCE HIS REGIME CONTROLS THE DISTRIBUTION OF GOODS

AMY PARKER
AMNESTY INTL

SADDAM HUSSEIN IS THE ONE RESPONSIBLE FOR THE SUFFERING OF HIS PEOPLE

JIM DALY

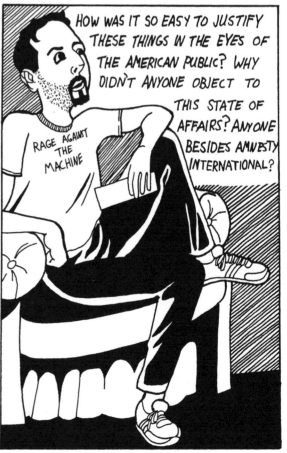

HOW WAS IT SO EASY TO JUSTIFY THESE THINGS IN THE EYES OF THE AMERICAN PUBLIC? WHY DIDN'T ANYONE OBJECT TO THIS STATE OF AFFAIRS? ANYONE BESIDES AMNESTY INTERNATIONAL?

NEGATIVE ATTITUDES TOWARDS ARABS AND MUSLIMS ARE VERY COMMON IN THE WEST WHERE ISLAM IS OFTEN VIEWED AS A THREAT OR COMPETITOR TO CHRISTIANITY.

IN 8TH GRADE, I HAD A TEACHER WHO TAUGHT US ABOUT THE BATTLE OF TOURS. THIS WAS A HISTORIC BATTLE BETWEEN ADVANCING ISLAMIC ARMIES OF THE IBERIAN PENINSULA AND THE CHRISTIAN FRANKS OF EUROPE IN THE YEAR 732.

IN THIS BATTLE, THE CHRISTIANS WON! AND DEFEATED THE ARAB MOSLEMS!

WHAT ARE MOSLEMS?

WELL, IT'S A DIFFERENT RELIGION, AN ARABIC ONE AND IF THEY WON THAT BATTLE WE WOULD ALL BE ARABS! CAN YOU IMAGINE? HA HA HA!

I GUESS SHE DIDN'T REALIZE THAT I WAS ALREADY AN ARAB.

WESTERN CULTURE IS REPLETE WITH STEREOTYPES ABOUT ARABS AND MUSLIMS. MANY OF THESE IMAGES COME FROM "1001 ARABIAN NIGHTS" AND HAVE BEEN REINFORCED THROUGHOUT THE WESTERN WORLD. THE MIDDLE EAST WAS OFTEN DEPICTED AS A LAND OF EXOTIC WONDER, FULL OF FLYING CARPETS, GENIES, AND LUSTY HAREMS.

SOME WORKS BY FRENCH PAINTERS JEAN AUGUSTE DOMINIQUE INGRES AND JEAN LEON GEROME ARE VERY GOOD EXAMPLES.

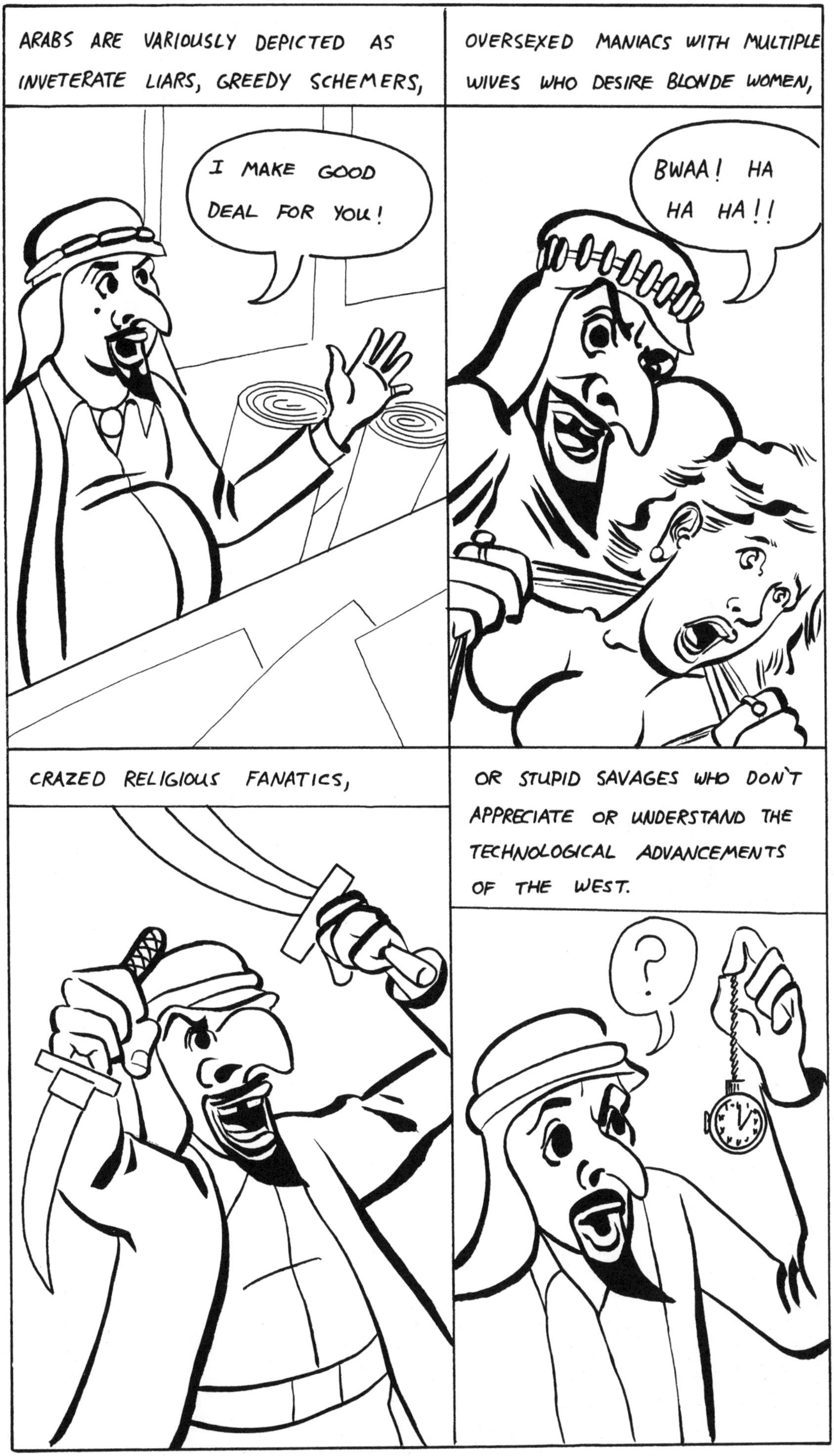
ARABS ARE VARIOUSLY DEPICTED AS INVETERATE LIARS, GREEDY SCHEMERS,
I MAKE GOOD DEAL FOR YOU!
OVERSEXED MANIACS WITH MULTIPLE WIVES WHO DESIRE BLONDE WOMEN,
BWAA! HA HA HA!!
CRAZED RELIGIOUS FANATICS,
OR STUPID SAVAGES WHO DON'T APPRECIATE OR UNDERSTAND THE TECHNOLOGICAL ADVANCEMENTS OF THE WEST.
?

RUDOLPH VALENTINO
The Sheik

THESE NEGATIVE IMAGES HAVE A LONG HISTORY THAT PERSIST IN AMERICA. BUT THEY REALLY STAND OUT IN THE MOVIES. EARLY EXAMPLES ARE RUDOLPH VALENTINO'S "THE SHEIK" (1921), "THE SON OF THE SHEIK" (1926), AND "THE THIEF OF BAGHDAD" (1940).

THE HOSTILITY IS STILL STRONG TODAY IN THE MODERN FILM INDUSTRY. THE 1996 MOVIE "COURAGE UNDER FIRE," STARRING DENZEL WASHINGTON AND MEG RYAN IS ABOUT A FEMALE SOLDIER RECEIVING THE MEDAL OF HONOR DURING THE FIRST GULF WAR. IT HAS A SCENE WHERE A SOLDIER DESCRIBES BEING PINNED DOWN BY IRAQI SOLDIERS.

AS IF THINGS WEREN'T BAD ENOUGH BEFORE, ONE OF THEIR T54s JOINS THE RAGHEADS ON THE RIDGE...

WE FIGURE IT'S ALL OVER AND THAT'S WHEN WE HEAR THE SOUND OF THE RESCUE TEAM, COBRAS, HUEYS...

AND A BIG ASS A10 THUNDERBOLT, I SWEAR I NEVER HEARD SUCH SWEET SOUNDS. NOW THE FUCKERS... I'M SORRY SIR, THE IRAQIS, ARE LETTING LOOSE WITH EVERYTHING THEY GOT...

NO, YOU WERE RIGHT THE FIRST TIME...

HA HA HA HA

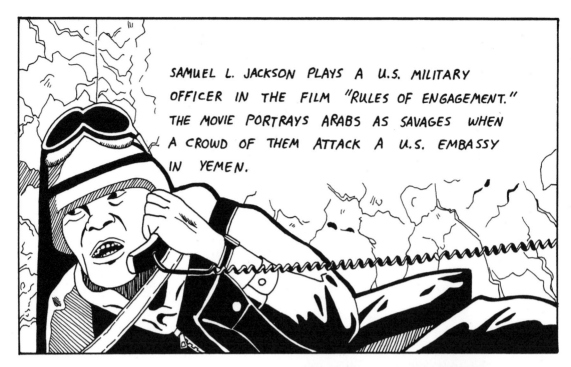

SAMUEL L. JACKSON PLAYS A U.S. MILITARY OFFICER IN THE FILM "RULES OF ENGAGEMENT." THE MOVIE PORTRAYS ARABS AS SAVAGES WHEN A CROWD OF THEM ATTACK A U.S. EMBASSY IN YEMEN.

JACKSON'S CHARACTER LEADS A SQUAD IN DEFENSE OF THE EMBASSY BY SHOOTING INTO THE CROWD OF ARABS, KILLING WOMEN AND CHILDREN. IT IS LATER REVEALED THE WOMEN HID RIFLES UNDER THEIR BURKAS. ONE OF THE SHOOTERS WAS EVEN A LITTLE GIRL.

AFTER BEING CHARGED WITH THE KILLINGS, JACKSON'S CHARACTER IS TRIED IN A SERIES OF RIVETING COURTROOM SCENES. WITH A POWERFUL DEFENSE LAWYER (PLAYED BY TOMMY LEE JONES) JACKSON IS VINDICATED OF THE SLAUGHTER.

THE SIEGE

"THE SIEGE" IS A MOVIE ABOUT ARAB AMERICANS COMMITTING TERRORISM IN NEW YORK CITY, RESULTING IN THE DECLARATION OF MARTIAL LAW AND MASS DETENTIONS OF ARAB AMERICANS BY THE GOVERNMENT. SLURS LIKE "TOWEL HEADS" ARE OPENLY USED AND THE MOST OMINOUS ASPECT OF THE FILM IS THAT THE "BAD GUYS" ARE HERE IN THE U.S. WHICH PUSHES THE SPECTER OF "SLEEPER CELLS" AND ENCOURAGES SUSPICION OF ARAB AMERICANS.

MOST OF THE ACTORS THAT PLAY THE ARABS LOOK LIKE STEREOTYPES, THEY ARE DARK SKINNED AND MOST ARE IN NEED OF A SHAVE OR ARE WEARING ISLAMIC OR TRADITIONAL DRESS.

THE MAIN TERRORIST (SAMIR) IS SHOWN PRAYING BEFORE HE STRAPS ON A BOMB ON HIS WAY TO KILL INNOCENT, PEACEFUL PROTESTORS WHO ARE OPPOSED TO MARTIAL LAW. THE MOTIVATIONS OF THE MINDLESS TERRORISTS ARE SO VAGUE THAT ONE CAN NOT HELP BUT SEE THEM AS SUBHUMAN.

43

IN THE MOVIE "THE DELTA FORCE" (1986) HEROES CHUCK NORRIS & LEE MARVIN TAKE OUT THE ARAB TRASH. IN THIS CLASSIC, LOOSELY BASED ON THE ACTUAL HIJACKING OF A TWA FLIGHT IN 1985, ARABS SEIZE A PLANE WITH AMERICAN PASSENGERS AND THE DELTA FORCE — A U.S. COUNTER TERRORISM UNIT SAVE THE DAY

THE LEAD TERRORIST (ABDUL) IS PLAYED BY A WELL TANNED ROBERT FORESTER, IN FACT ALMOST NONE OF THE ARABS ARE ACTUALLY PLAYED BY ARABS. THE ARABS ARE SHOWN AS RUTHLESSLY EVIL, THEY EVEN TARGET THE JEWISH PASSENGERS ON THE PLANE.

ALLAH AKBAR!!

IN SOLIDARITY WITH THE JEWS A CHRISTIAN PRIEST WHO IS ON THE PLANE DECLARES:

I'M JEWISH, JUST LIKE JESUS CHRIST!

IN THIS REVENGE FANTASY THE SWARTHY, INEPT ARABS GET SLAUGHTERED EN MASSE BY THE DELTA FORCE

THE ANTI-ARAB STEREOTYPES ARE SO INGRAINED IN AMERICAN AND WESTERN CULTURE THAT THEY OFTEN GO UNNOTICED AND EVEN APPEAR IN SEEMINGLY INNOCUOUS POP-ART. THE STAR WARS FILMS BY GEORGE LUCAS ARE A GOOD CASE IN POINT.

THE TUSKEN RAIDERS OR "SAND PEOPLE" THAT APPEAR IN THE FILMS ARE CLEARLY REPRESENTATIVE OF ARAB NOMADS. THEY ARE SAVAGES WHO ROAM THE SPARSE DESERT PLANET OF TATOOINE AND ARE MINDLESSLY VIOLENT AND HOSTILE.

THE JABBA THE HUTT CHARACTER WHO ALSO INHABITS THIS PLANET IS AN EVIL CRIME LEADER WHO LOUNGES IN HIS LAIR WITH HIS HAREM OF SLAVE GIRLS. HE EVEN SMOKES A WATER PIPE.

AND FINALLY, THE WATTO CHARACTER (AGAIN FROM TATOOINE) — A GREEDY, HOOK-NOSED MERCHANT WHO IS CUNNING AND DUPLICITOUS. HE EVEN HAS STUBBLE ON HIS FACE AND SPEAKS WITH AN ARABIC ACCENT.

45

OUT OF CURIOSITY I WENT TO SEE "TRUE LIES" A JAMES CAMERON FILM ABOUT ARAB TERRORISTS MENACING THE U.S. IN THIS ACTION PACKED EXTRAVAGANZA ARNOLD SCHWARZENEGGER PLAYS A SECRET AGENT FOR THE GOVERNMENT AS HE CONFRONTS THE TERRORISTS.

EVERY TIME AN ARAB WAS KILLED OR "TAKEN DOWN" A GROUP OF YOUNG GUYS BEHIND ME WOULD ROAR.

WHEEW!! YEAH!! THAT'S AWESOME!!

HA HA HA YEAH, TH WAS COO

HELL YES!! HA HA DID YOU SEE THAT?

YEAH!! SHOOT THAT FUCKER!!

HA HA HA HA HA HA

THOSE MOVIES ARE A MERE SAMPLING OF HOW THE MEDIA DEPICTS ARABS AND THE MIDDLE EAST

WHILE I WAS IN COLLEGE I BECAME INCREASINGLY BOTHERED BY THESE NEGATIVE DEPICTIONS. DURING THIS PERIOD I WANTED TO KNOW MORE ABOUT MY HERITAGE SO I READ MUCH ABOUT THE MIDDLE EAST

IN THE NEWSPAPERS AND MAGAZINES OR ON TELEVISION NEWS "ARABS" OR "ISLAM" IS USUALLY SYNONYMOUS WITH VIOLENCE AND TERRORISM

WHENEVER THE MIDDLE EAST IS COVERED IN THE NEWS WE INVARIABLY SEE THE IMAGES OF CRAZED MUSLIM MOBS WIELDING MACHINE GUNS

OR MARCHING WITH SCARY MASKS

OR THE UBIQUITOUS CHILD HOLDING A GUN

OR AMERICAN FLAGS BURNING

IF AMERICANS WANT TO KNOW MORE ABOUT THE MIDDLE EAST THEY HAVE TO RELY ON "EXPERTS" WHO ARE CLEARLY BIASED AGAINST ARABS AND ISLAM. FOR EXAMPLE, ONE OF THE MOST POPULAR BOOKS ABOUT THE MIDDLE EAST AND THE ARAB-ISRAELI CONFLICT IS "FROM BEIRUT TO JERUSALEM" WRITTEN BY NEW YORK TIMES REPORTER THOMAS FRIEDMAN WHO EXPLICITLY STATES HIS ZIONIST ALLEGIANCE AND DESCRIBES BEIRUT AS A "SKINNER BOX."

ANOTHER SO-CALLED EXPERT ON THE MIDDLE EAST IS JUDITH MILLER WHO WROTE THE BOOK, "GOD HAS NINETY NINE NAMES" AND SUPPORTED THE 2003 INVASION OF IRAQ IN HER CAPACITY AS A JOURNALIST FOR THE NEW YORK TIMES. SHE ALSO MAKES CLEAR HER PRO-ISRAEL VIEWS AND GOES ABOUT DESCRIBING THE "MILITANT ISLAM" OF THE ARAB WORLD, COMPLETE WITH EXECUTIONS AND MEDIEVAL PUNISHMENTS. I WONDER WHY SHE DIDN'T JUST CALL IT "TERRORIST ISLAM?"

FINALLY, WE HAVE RENOWNED PRINCETON PROFESSOR BERNARD LEWIS, AN EXPERT ON ARABS AND THE MIDDLE EAST. CRITICIZED AS AN ORIENTALIST BY EDWARD SAID, HIS SCHOLARSHIP IS DEDICATED TO DEMONSTRATING THE TOTAL BACKWARDNESS OF ARABS AND MUSLIMS AND THE SUPERIORITY OF THE WEST. LEWIS IS THE AUTHOR OF A NUMBER OF BOOKS AND ESSAYS ON ARABS AND ISLAM AND IS VERY INFLUENTIAL IN THE FIELD. IN FACT HE IS THE ONE WHO CAME UP WITH THE TERM "CLASH OF CIVILIZATIONS."

THESE IMAGES REINFORCED THE STEREOTYPES OF ARABS AS MANIACS AND WHETHER I LIKED IT OR NOT I WAS INCLUDED IN THAT CATEGORY. TRYING TO AVOID THAT FACT WAS POINTLESS.

I WAS BORN IN BEIRUT AND GROWING UP, THE CITY OF BEIRUT WAS ASSOCIATED WITH VIOLENCE AND TERRORISM. REACTIONS WERE USUALLY THE SAME WHENEVER SOMEONE DISCOVERED WHERE I WAS BORN. MY HIGH SCHOOL COUNSELOR OFFERED HIS OPINION UPON READING MY FILE:

AT JOB INTERVIEWS I GOT SIMILAR REACTIONS:

IN THE AFTERMATH OF 9/11 MY EMPLOYMENT WAS ACTUALLY HELD UP WHEN I GOT A JOB AT MY SCHOOL BECAUSE I WASN'T BORN IN THE U.S. I WAS TOLD TO PROVIDE PROOF OF MY STATUS.

I GAVE MY SOCIAL SECURITY CARD, DRIVER'S LICENSE, SCHOOL ID, BUT THIS WAS NOT ENOUGH, THEY DEMANDED A GREEN CARD.

I RECEIVED MY GREEN CARD WHEN MY PARENTS ARRIVED TO THE U.S. MORE THAN 25 YEARS AGO AND IT HAS MY BABY PICTURE ON IT.

SO I HAD TO APPLY FOR A TEMPORARY GREEN CARD FROM IMMIGRATION SERVICES, THE SCARY PHOTO ON IT MUST HAVE CREATED EVEN MORE ALARM AT HUMAN RESOURCES.

THEN THEY DEMANDED A BIRTH CERTIFICATE SO I HAD TO SEND TO LEBANON FOR ONE. IT WAS STRANGE WHEN IT ARRIVED, HERE WAS A DOCUMENT THAT'S SUPPOSED TO PROVE MY BIRTH, MY EXISTENCE YET IT WAS JUST A 5" BY 8" PIECE OF PAPER IN ARABIC WRITING THAT I COULDN'T EVEN READ. HOW MUCH USE COULD IT BE TO MY EMPLOYERS?

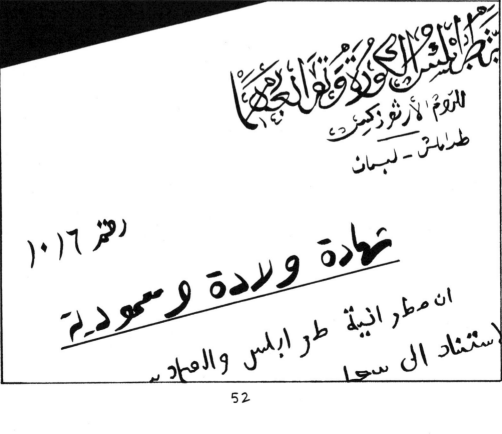

IT WASN'T UNTIL MY BOSS FOUND OUT I WAS WORKING FOR OVER A WEEK WITHOUT PAY THAT HE CALLED UP HUMAN RESOURCES AND STRAIGHTENED THINGS OUT.

LISTEN, I KNOW THESE ARE TROUBLING TIMES BUT I THINK THESE PRECAUTIONS ARE A LITTLE MUCH...

LATER I FOUND OUT THAT THE DEMANDS THEY MADE OF ME WERE ILLEGAL. PROVIDING A SOCIAL SECURITY CARD AND A DRIVER'S LICENSE WAS SUFFICIENT ACCORDING TO THE EMPLOYEE HANDBOOK AND THE LAW.

THIS WHOLE BIZARRE SCENARIO HAPPENED BECAUSE I WAS ONLY A YEAR OLD WHEN MY PARENTS CAME FROM LEBANON. HAD IT BEEN JUST A YEAR SOONER I WOULD HAVE BEEN BORN IN THE U.S.

53

MY MOTHER CAME FROM EGYPT TO LEBANON WHERE SHE MET MY FATHER AND THEY MARRIED THERE. LIFE WAS OK SINCE MY DAD HAD A VENDING MACHINE BUSINESS.

I WAS BORN IN THE MIDST OF THE CIVIL WAR IN BEIRUT AND MY MOTHER FEARED FOR OUR LIVES.

THE WAR BROKE OUT IN 1975 AND MY PARENTS FLED IN 1979, MY TWO OLDER SISTERS WERE JUST LITTLE GIRLS AT THE TIME.

THE LEBANESE STATE, (LIKE MOST ARAB STATES) WAS CREATED BY EUROPEAN COLONIAL POWERS AFTER THE COLLAPSE OF THE OTTOMAN EMPIRE.

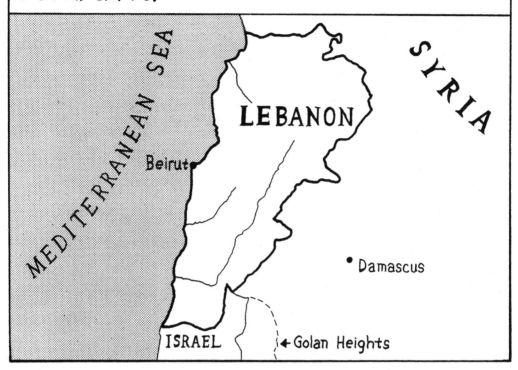

LEBANON HOSTS A VARIETY OF RELIGIOUS GROUPINGS WHO FOUND REFUGE IN THIS MOUNTAINOUS AREA THROUGHOUT THE CENTURIES. IN FACT LEBANON IS THE ONLY ARAB COUNTRY THAT HAS A LARGE CHRISTIAN MINORITY.

I TRIED EXPLAINING THE FACT THAT THERE ARE SUCH THINGS AS ARAB CHRISTIANS ONCE TO A FRIEND BUT HE DIDN'T UNDERSTAND.

YOU MEAN LIKE JEWS FOR JESUS?

WHEN LEBANON WAS BORN IN 1943 THE COUNTRY HAD A CHRISTIAN MAJORITY BUT IT ALSO HAD A SIGNIFICANT MUSLIM MINORITY AND A POWER SHARING AGREEMENT WAS DEVISED TO FAVOR THE CHRISTIANS. FOR A WHILE LEBANON WAS SEEN AS A MODEL OF TOLERANCE AND PLURALISM IN THE ARAB WORLD.

SOON THE MUSLIMS BECAME THE MAJORITY AND THE INFLUX OF PALESTINIAN MUSLIM REFUGEES AFTER THE CREATION OF THE STATE OF ISRAEL ADDED TO THE TENSE SITUATION. THE MUSLIM MAJORITY DEMANDED AN END TO THE OLD POLITICAL ARRANGEMENT AND MORE POWER, THE CHRISTIANS RESISTED AND THE CIVIL WAR BEGAN.

THE LEBANESE CIVIL WAR WAS A VIOLENT AND HORRIFIC WAR RESULTING IN 150,000 PEOPLE KILLED – MOSTLY CIVILIANS. THE COSMOPOLITAN AND BEAUTIFUL SEASIDE CAPITAL OF BEIRUT WAS DESTROYED AS RIVAL MILITIAS USED HIGH RISES DOWNTOWN TO VOLLEY SHELLS AT EACH OTHER.

ISRAEL'S INVASION IN 1982 INTENSIFIED THE CARNAGE ESPECIALLY WHEN THE ISRAELIS INDISCRIMINATELY BOMBED WEST BEIRUT AND LAID SIEGE TO IT IN ORDER TO DRIVE OUT THE PALESTINIAN LIBERATION ORGANIZATION WHICH WAS HEADQUARTERED THERE.

EVENTUALLY YASIR ARAFAT AND HIS MEN WERE DRIVEN OUT IN AN AGREEMENT WITH THE INTERNATIONAL COMMUNITY INCLUDING THE U.S. WHICH SENT THE MARINES TO OVERSEE THE DEPARTURE OF THE PLO.

BUT SOON AFTER THE DEPARTURE OF THE PLO THE NEWLY INSTALLED PRO-ISRAELI PRESIDENT BASHIR GEYAMEL WAS ASSASSINATED IN A HUGE EXPLOSION.

WHICH RESULTED IN THE MASSACRE OF HUNDREDS OF PALESTINIAN REFUGEES IN THE SHATILA AND SABRA CAMPS OUTSIDE OF BEIRUT. THE ISRAELI ARMY SURROUNDED THE CAMPS AND THEN TRUCKED IN GEYAMEL'S FOLLOWERS OSTENSIBLY TO KILL ANY REMAINING PALESTINIAN FIGHTERS BUT THERE WERE NONE AND WHAT RESULTED WAS AN ATROCITY.

THE WAR OFFICIALLY ENDED IN 1990 AND SINCE THEN A SEMBLANCE OF NORMALCY SEEMS TO BE RETURNING BUT THE POLITICAL SITUATION THERE IS STILL UNCERTAIN.

MY UNCLE ALREADY LEFT FOR THE U.S. YEARS BEFORE MY FAMILY FOLLOWED. AN ECCENTRIC MAN, MY UNCLE WAS OF ALL THINGS A HAIRDRESSER WHO DECIDED TO SETTLE IN CHICAGO WHERE HE BOUGHT A HOUSE IN THE SUBURBS. SOON AFTER OUR ARRIVAL HE DECIDED TO LEAVE TO CALIFORNIA — I'VE ONLY SEEN HIM ONCE SINCE.

AFTER YEARS OF HARD WORK AND SAVING, MY PARENTS WERE ABLE TO BUY A HOUSE IN THE SAME SUBURB MY UNCLE LEFT. PUTTING 50,000 DOLLARS DOWN IN CASH WE WERE NOW THE STRANGE NEW NEIGHBORS IN THE MOSTLY WHITE NEIGHBORHOOD.

THIS WAS AROUND 1983 OR SO AND OUR NEIGHBORS QUICKLY WELCOMED US TO THE NEIGHBORHOOD.

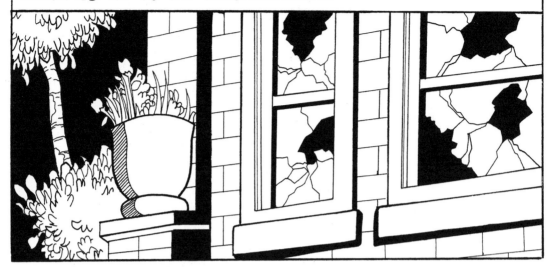

OUR BACKYARD WAS CONNECTED TO THE PROPERTY OF A NEIGHBOR AND MY SIBLINGS AND I WERE OUT PLAYING ONE DAY AND WE VENTURED ONTO OUR NEIGHBOR'S PROPERTY.

THE MAN NEXT DOOR DIDN'T TAKE TOO KINDLY TO OUR TRESPASS SO HE CAME OUT TO LET US KNOW.

THE NEIGHBORHOOD KIDS WOULD MAKE FUN OF US USING SLURS THAT COULD ONLY HAVE COME FROM THEIR PARENTS' INFLUENCE.

TERRORISTS!!

SAND NIGGERS!

CAMEL JOCKEYS!!!

HA HA HA HA

MY SIBLINGS AND I DIDN'T KNOW HOW TO REACT ESPECIALLY SINCE WE DIDN'T KNOW WHAT THEY MEANT. MY BROTHER ASKED ME:

HEY TOUFIC, WHAT IS A CAMEL JOCKEY??

I DON'T KNOW.

AT THE TIME I JUST IMAGINED A HORSE JOCKEY ON A CAMEL.

ALSO, AT FIRST WE WONDERED:

WHY ARE THEY CALLING US NIGGERS? WE'RE NOT BLACK.

MY BIGGEST AGGRAVATION WAS WHEN I WOULD BE CALLED THE WRONG RACIST NAMES:

HEY YOU FUCKING SPIC!!!

HEY AYATOLLAH!

WITH THE POPULARITY OF THE TV SITCOM "THE SIMPSONS" I HAD TO CONTEND WITH YET ANOTHER CRASS STEREOTYPE WHICH WAS REGULARLY FOISTED UPON ME.

HEY HINDU!

WHAT'S SO FRUSTRATING ABOUT ALL THIS IS THAT AMERICANS DON'T EVEN KNOW WHO THEY HATE. SINCE THERE IS SO MUCH CONFUSION AND IGNORANCE IT MAY BE USEFUL TO EXPLAIN WHAT AN ARAB ACTUALLY IS.

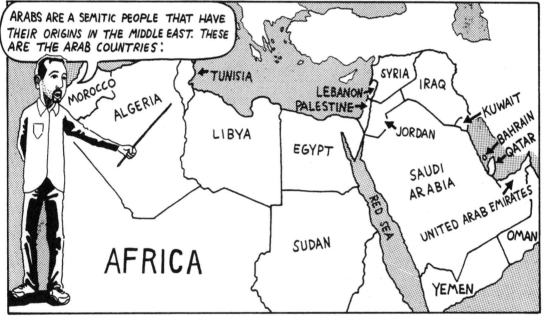

ARABS ARE A SEMITIC PEOPLE THAT HAVE THEIR ORIGINS IN THE MIDDLE EAST. THESE ARE THE ARAB COUNTRIES:

MOROCCO
ALGERIA
TUNISIA
LIBYA
EGYPT
SYRIA
IRAQ
LEBANON
PALESTINE
JORDAN
KUWAIT
BAHRAIN
QATAR
SAUDI ARABIA
UNITED ARAB EMIRATES
OMAN
RED SEA
SUDAN
AFRICA
YEMEN

HEBREW, SYRIAC, ARAMAIC, AND ARABIC ARE SOME OF THE SEMITIC LANGUAGES THAT WERE OR ARE SPOKEN BY THE PEOPLES OF THE REGION.

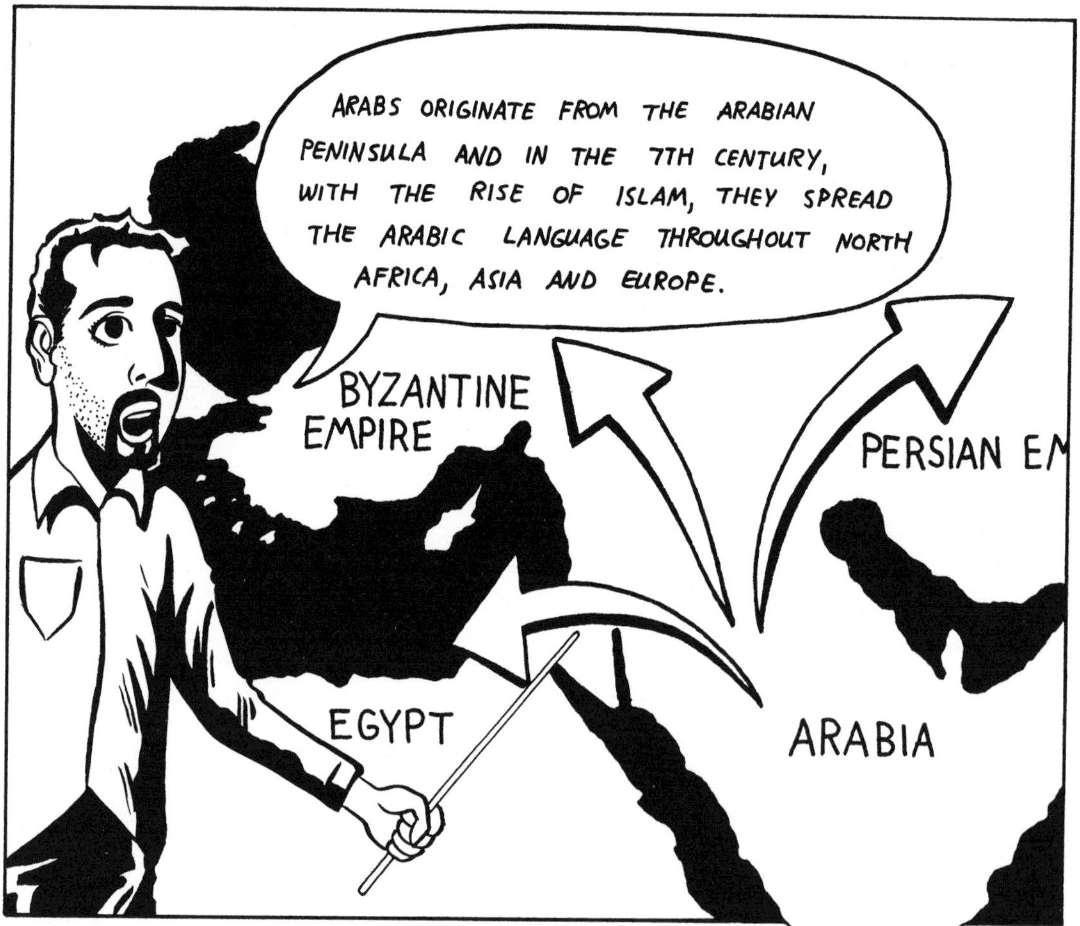
ARABS ORIGINATE FROM THE ARABIAN PENINSULA AND IN THE 7TH CENTURY, WITH THE RISE OF ISLAM, THEY SPREAD THE ARABIC LANGUAGE THROUGHOUT NORTH AFRICA, ASIA AND EUROPE.
BYZANTINE EMPIRE
PERSIAN EM
EGYPT
ARABIA

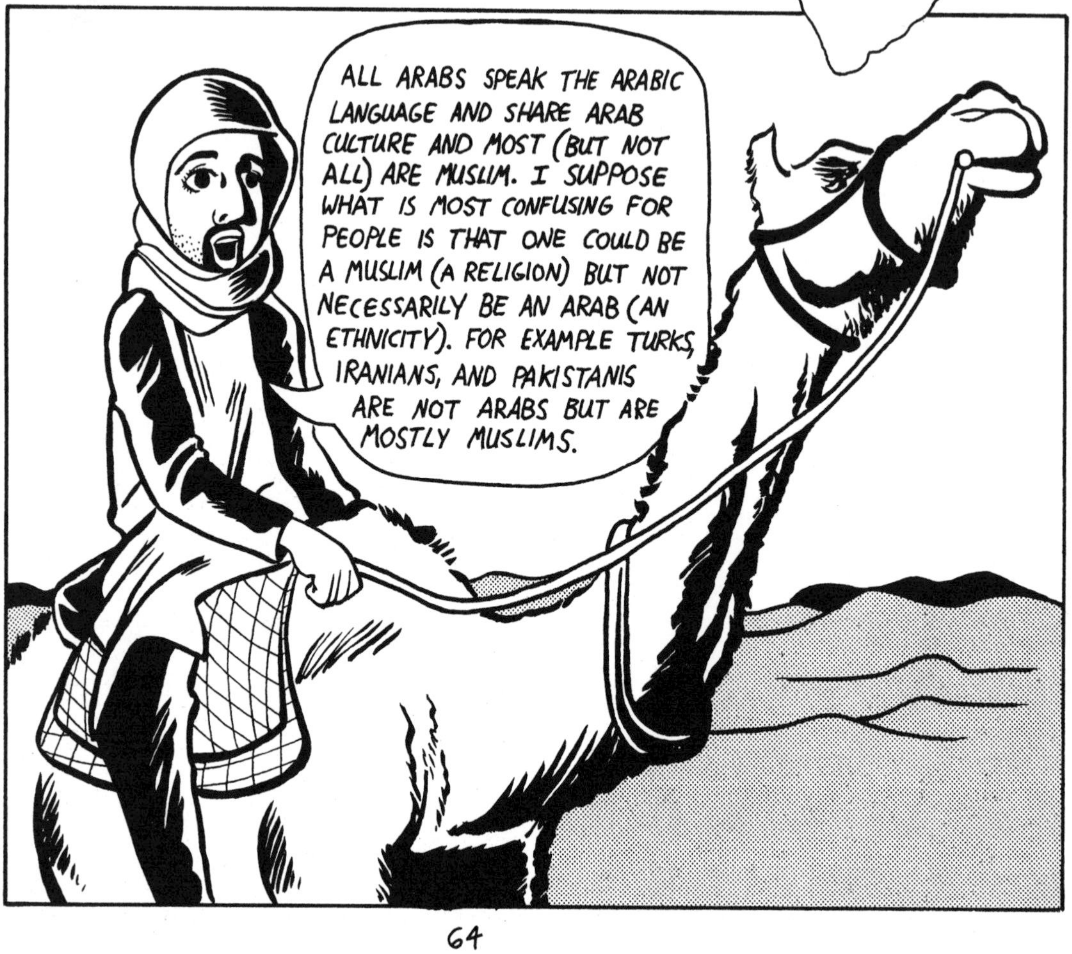
ALL ARABS SPEAK THE ARABIC LANGUAGE AND SHARE ARAB CULTURE AND MOST (BUT NOT ALL) ARE MUSLIM. I SUPPOSE WHAT IS MOST CONFUSING FOR PEOPLE IS THAT ONE COULD BE A MUSLIM (A RELIGION) BUT NOT NECESSARILY BE AN ARAB (AN ETHNICITY). FOR EXAMPLE TURKS, IRANIANS, AND PAKISTANIS ARE NOT ARABS BUT ARE MOSTLY MUSLIMS.

SO THE DREADED AYATOLLAH KHOMEINI WAS A DEVOUT MUSLIM BUT NOT AN ARAB BUT IN FACT AN IRANIAN.

AND PRESIDENT PERVEZ MUSHARRAF OF PAKISTAN IS ALSO A MUSLIM BUT AGAIN, NOT AN ARAB BUT A PAKISTANI.

AND MUSTAFA KEMAL (THE FOUNDER OF MODERN TURKEY) IS A MUSLIM AS WELL BUT HE IS A TURK NOT AN ARAB.

WHAT ADDS TO THE CONFUSION IS THAT SOME ISLAMIC COUNTRIES (LIKE IRAN) USE THE ARABIC SCRIPT TO WRITE THEIR LANGUAGES. ALSO THE HOLY BOOK OF ISLAM, THE QURAN, IS WRITTEN IN ARABIC AND DEVOUT MUSLIMS MUST LEARN TO READ IT IN THAT LANGUAGE.

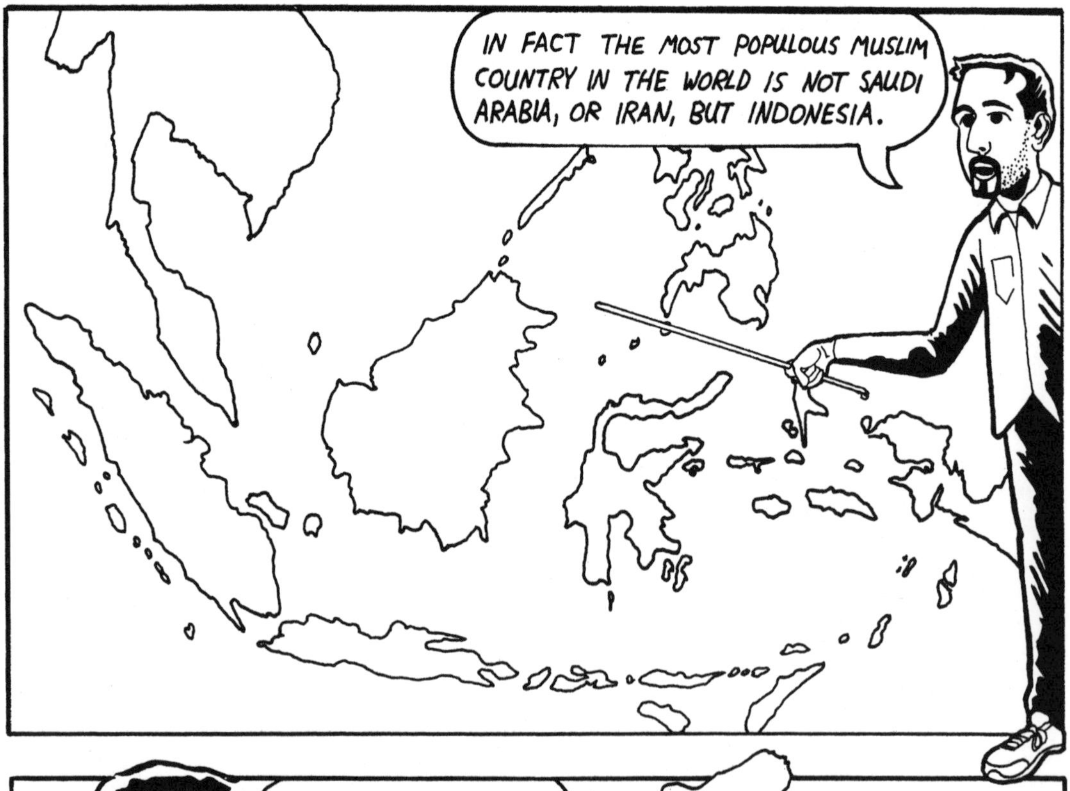
IN FACT THE MOST POPULOUS MUSLIM COUNTRY IN THE WORLD IS NOT SAUDI ARABIA, OR IRAN, BUT INDONESIA.

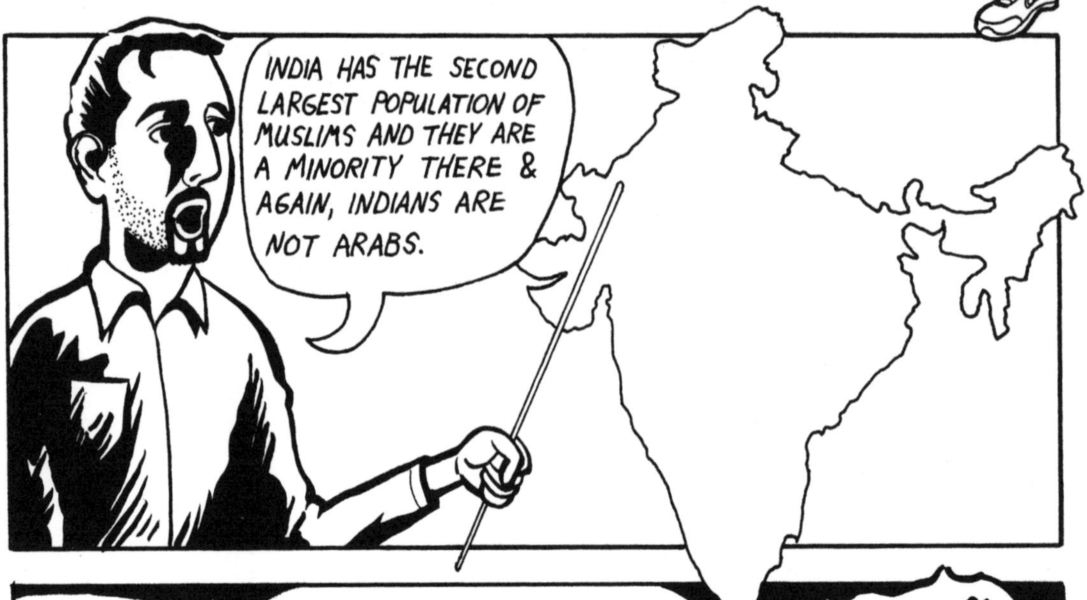
INDIA HAS THE SECOND LARGEST POPULATION OF MUSLIMS AND THEY ARE A MINORITY THERE & AGAIN, INDIANS ARE NOT ARABS.

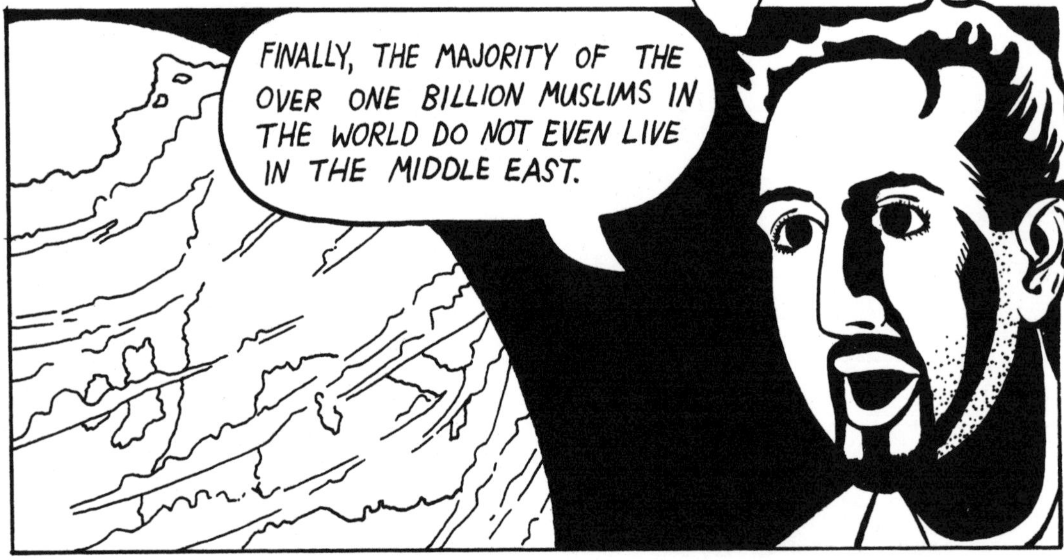
FINALLY, THE MAJORITY OF THE OVER ONE BILLION MUSLIMS IN THE WORLD DO NOT EVEN LIVE IN THE MIDDLE EAST.

AT THE END OF THE IRAN-IRAQ WAR A TEACHER OF MINE SAID:

IRANIANS AND IRAQIS SHOULD NOT FIGHT, THEY ARE BOTH ARABS SO IT'S LIKE A CIVIL WAR.

I HATED IT WHEN HE WOULD PRONOUNCE ARAB WORDS LIKE IRAQ.

LET'S TALK ABOUT I-RACK.

IT'S AN ENDEMIC PROBLEM, TODAY WHEN AMERICAN OFFICIALS OR SOLDIERS SAY THINGS LIKE:

WE'RE HERE TO HELP THE I-RACKEES.

I JUST CAN'T HELP THINKING THEY CAN'T EVEN SAY THE NAME OF THE COUNTRY THEY ARE SUPPOSEDLY HELPING.

MORONS....

I-RACK BELONGS TO THE I-RACKEES.

CONSIDERING THE EDUCATIONAL SYSTEM IN THE U.S. IT IS NOT SURPRISING THAT THE AVERAGE AMERICAN WOULD BE IGNORANT OF FOREIGN CULTURES AND SOCIETIES. THE MISPRONUNCIATION OF FOREIGN WORDS COULD ALSO BE EXCUSED EVEN IF HIGH LEVEL GOVERNMENT OFFICIALS RESPONSIBLE FOR LIFE AND DEATH DECISIONS DO IT.

HOWEVER, WHEN THE LEADER OF THE UNITED STATES (WITH THE GOAL OF TRANSFORMATION OF THE MIDDLE EAST) DEMONSTRATES IGNORANCE OF THE REGION, IT IS A SIGN OF TROUBLE.

IT WOULDN'T BE SO TROUBLESOME IF THERE WERE NO DECLARATIONS OF SOLIDARITY AND CONCERN FOR ARABS AND MUSLIMS. USUALLY, WHEN ONE HAS CONCERN FOR A GROUP, THERE IS AT LEAST SOME FAMILIARITY WITH THAT GROUP. SO IT IS HARD TO TAKE PRONOUNCEMENTS OF ALTRUISM SERIOUSLY WHEN THERE IS NO KNOWLEDGE ABOUT THE PEOPLE WHO ARE TO BE HELPED.

MAYBE THE MOST DRAMATIC ILLUSTRATION OF THIS CONTRADICTION HAPPENED IN MARCH 2006. WHILE SPEAKING IN INDIA PRIOR TO DEPARTING FOR A VISIT TO PAKISTAN, PRESIDENT GEORGE W. BUSH REVEALED HIS LACK OF KNOWLEDGE OF THE MIDDLE EAST AND ITS PEOPLES WHEN HE SAID:

I BELIEVE THAT A PROSPEROUS, DEMOCRATIC PAKISTAN WILL BE A STEADFAST PARTNER FOR AMERICA, A PEACEFUL NEIGHBOR FOR INDIA AND A FORCE FOR FREEDOM AND MODERATION IN THE ARAB WORLD.

I HAD A FEW MUSLIM & MIDDLE EASTERN FRIENDS AND THEY RAN THE GAMUT WHEN IT CAME TO THEIR IDENTITY. MY IRANIAN FRIEND, HAMID, WOULD BE AN EXAMPLE:

HE INSISTED ON BEING CALLED "HARRY" AND WENT OUT OF HIS WAY TO CONCEAL HIS ETHNICITY. HE ALWAYS WORE TRENDY CLOTHES AND EVEN COLORED HIS HAIR BLONDE.

HEY, SO WHAT NATIONALITY ARE YOU?

I'M PERSIAN.

YOU MEAN IRANIAN?

NO, NO, I'M PERSIAN, PERSIAN!

HE CULTIVATED A PUNK-HIPPIE LOOK THAT I ATTEMPTED TO EMULATE BUT IT DIDN'T WORK OUT.

MARILYN MANSON

WHEN ARIEL SHARON WENT TO THE TEMPLE MOUNT IN 2000 SPARKING THE SECOND INTIFADA IN ISRAEL/PALESTINE I TRIED TO ENGAGE IN A DISCUSSION WITH HAMID.

HEY MAN DO YOU BELIEVE WHAT'S HAPPENING IN PALESTINE?

WHAT???

I MEAN ALL THE VIOLENCE, YOU KNOW, THE AL AQSA INTIFADA.

LOOK MAN, I DON'T GIVE A SHIT ABOUT THOSE FUCKING TERRORISTS. THEY COULD KILL EACH OTHER FOR ALL I CARE.

WHAT DO YOU MEAN?

THAT STUFF DOESN'T CONCERN ME, I'M NOT AN A-RAB.

YEAH, BUT YOU'RE MUSLIM.

NO WAY MAN, I'M JUST SPIRITUAL— DON'T CALL ME THAT MAN. LISTEN LET'S JUST WATCH THE GAME OK?

I ALSO HAD A PALESTINIAN FRIEND, AHMED, WHO WAS THE POLAR OPPOSITE OF HAMID. AT SOME POINT HE BECAME DEEPLY RELIGIOUS AND INSISTED ON DRESSING IN TRADITIONAL ISLAMIC GARB.

HE WAS ADAMANT ABOUT ALL OF HIS RELIGIOUS OBLIGATIONS LIKE PRAYING FIVE TIMES A DAY.

YOU WANT TO GO TO THE MOVIES??

OKAY BUT I HAVE TO PRAY FIRST.

HE ALSO BECAME A VOCIFEROUS CRITIC OF U.S. POLICIES IN THE MIDDLE EAST.

MUSLIMS HAVE TO UNITE AGAINST ALL THESE ASSAULTS ON US. YOU KNOW MAN, THIS COUNTRY GIVES ALL THIS MONEY TO ISRAEL SO IT CAN MURDER OUR CHILDREN AND TAKE OUR LAND!!

AHMED HAD A POINT — THE U.S. HAS HISTORICALLY SUPPORTED THE STATE OF ISRAEL AND THAT RELATIONSHIP HAS BECOME A CORNERSTONE IN U.S. FOREIGN POLICY. THE U.S. UNDER TRUMAN WAS THE FIRST COUNTRY TO RECOGNIZE ISRAEL AFTER IT WAS CREATED IN MAY OF 1948.

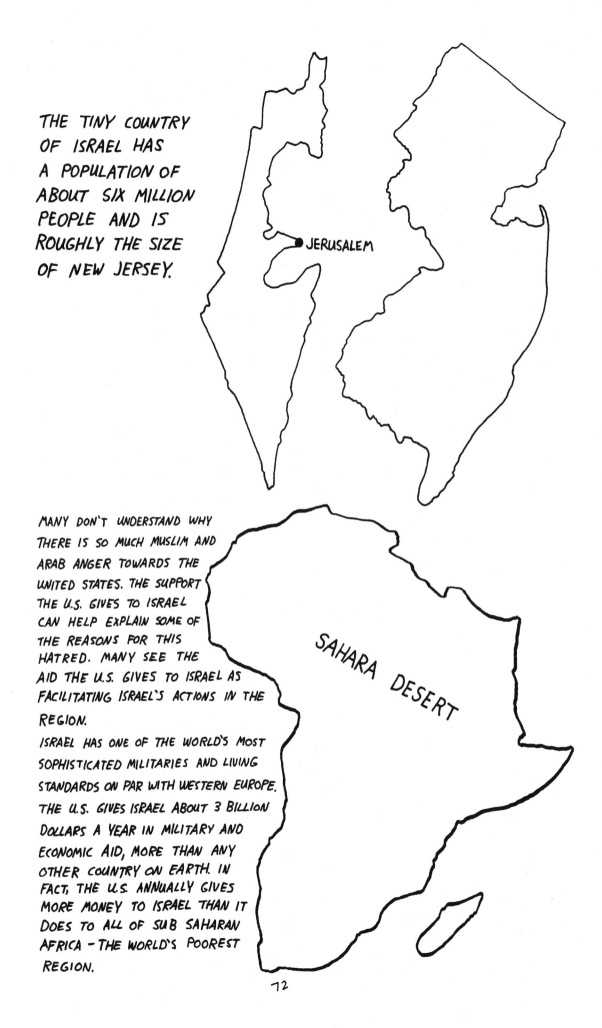

THE TINY COUNTRY OF ISRAEL HAS A POPULATION OF ABOUT SIX MILLION PEOPLE AND IS ROUGHLY THE SIZE OF NEW JERSEY.

• JERUSALEM

MANY DON'T UNDERSTAND WHY THERE IS SO MUCH MUSLIM AND ARAB ANGER TOWARDS THE UNITED STATES. THE SUPPORT THE U.S. GIVES TO ISRAEL CAN HELP EXPLAIN SOME OF THE REASONS FOR THIS HATRED. MANY SEE THE AID THE U.S. GIVES TO ISRAEL AS FACILITATING ISRAEL'S ACTIONS IN THE REGION.

ISRAEL HAS ONE OF THE WORLD'S MOST SOPHISTICATED MILITARIES AND LIVING STANDARDS ON PAR WITH WESTERN EUROPE. THE U.S. GIVES ISRAEL ABOUT 3 BILLION DOLLARS A YEAR IN MILITARY AND ECONOMIC AID, MORE THAN ANY OTHER COUNTRY ON EARTH. IN FACT, THE U.S. ANNUALLY GIVES MORE MONEY TO ISRAEL THAN IT DOES TO ALL OF SUB SAHARAN AFRICA - THE WORLD'S POOREST REGION.

SAHARA DESERT

72

YOU HAVE TO WATCH WHAT YOU SAY THESE DAYS AHMED, ESPECIALLY YOU. I WOULDN'T BE SURPRISED IF THE FBI IS TAPPING YOUR PHONE.

I DON'T CARE! I'M NOT AFRAID, I HAVE THE RIGHT, NO THE DUTY TO SPEAK OUT! HEY, WHY DON'T YOU COME TO THE MOSQUE?

I ADMIRED AHMED AND THE COURAGE OF HIS CONVICTIONS AND HIS STAUNCH ADHERENCE TO THE MORAL AND ETHICAL CODE THAT HE LIVED BY.

MAYBE LATER.

ESPECIALLY BECAUSE IT WAS SOMETHING I COULD NEVER DO.

HE WOULD OFTEN GET STARES FROM PASSERSBY WHEN WE WERE IN PUBLIC TOGETHER. I KNOW HE ENJOYED FREAKING PEOPLE OUT.

WHAT ARE YOU LOOKING AT?? YEAH, I'M MUSLIM SO WHAT??

LAILA, MY JORDANIAN FRIEND, NEVER SPOKE ABOUT RELIGION OR CARED ABOUT POLITICS FOR THE FIRST FEW YEARS I KNEW HER.

BUT SHE CHANGED AROUND THE TIME OF THE SEPTEMBER II ATTACKS, ALL OF THE SUDDEN SHE BEGAN WEARING A HIJAB.

WHAT'S WITH THE HIJAB?

YOU KNOW, JUST TRYING TO BE MORE DEVOUT.

SINCE WHEN?

WELL SINCE I WAS A KID BEING MUSLIM WAS LIKE EMBARRASSING BUT NOW WITH ALL THE STUFF HAPPENING, IT'S CRAZIER.

EXACTLY, SO WHY ADVERTISE YOUR RELIGION?

WHAT? LOOK I HAVE EVERY RIGHT TO BE A MUSLIM AND WEAR WHAT I WANT. I MEAN LOOK AT WHAT THEY ARE DOING TO US – THEY BOMB US, SANCTION US, TAKE OUR LAND, MAKE US REFUGEES, AND THEN THEY TRY TO MAKE US ASHAMED OF WHO WE ARE?

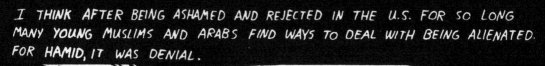

I THINK AFTER BEING ASHAMED AND REJECTED IN THE U.S. FOR SO LONG MANY YOUNG MUSLIMS AND ARABS FIND WAYS TO DEAL WITH BEING ALIENATED. FOR HAMID, IT WAS DENIAL.

I AM AN AMERICAN AND PROUD OF IT. I SPEAK ENGLISH, I EAT HOT DOGS, I LIKE SPORTS, AND MY NAME IS HARRY! I'M NOT ONE OF THOSE CRAZY TERRORISTS!!

FOR AHMED IT WAS A REJECTION OF THE REJECTION.

HOW CAN I BE PART OF A SOCIETY THAT REJECTS WHO I AM? THAT SUPPORTS THE KILLING AND OPPRESSION OF MY PEOPLE? WHAT KIND OF PERSON WOULD I BE IF I SAT SILENTLY?

AND LAILA ALSO EMBRACED HER HERITAGE AS A SIGN OF PROTEST

LOOK, IF THEY HAVE A PROBLEM WITH ME THEN THEY CAN SAY IT TO MY FACE. I'M PROUD OF WHO I AM.

I HAD NO IDEA WHO I WAS. AMERICAN? ARAB? I SPOKE ENGLISH PERFECTLY AND GREW UP HERE IN THE MIDST OF THIS CULTURE BUT I DID NOT BELONG HERE AND I KNEW THAT.

THE STRUGGLE TO FIND AN IDENTITY AS ARAB OR MUSLIM OR MIDDLE EASTERN IS BOUND UP WITH THE NEED FOR ACCEPTANCE IN AMERICAN SOCIETY.

THROUGHOUT MY LIFE I HAVE BEEN CONSTANTLY REMINDED HOW "SCARY" I LOOK TO OTHERS.

MY FRIEND WORKED IN THE COLLEGE ART GALLERY AND I VISITED HER AT CLOSING TIME. A WOMAN WAS WORRIED ENOUGH BY THE SIGHT OF ME TO ADVISE MY FRIEND:

EXCUSE ME, THAT MAN LOOKS VERY SUSPICIOUS, I THINK YOU SHOULD CALL CAMPUS SECURITY.

WHAT? NO, HE IS A FRIEND OF MINE.

WHO WE ARE IS IN LARGE PART DETERMINED BY HOW WE ARE VIEWED BY OTHERS AND APPARENTLY, "SCARY" OR THREATENING IS HOW MOST AMERICANS SEE ME.

THE BIZARRE FEAR THAT MY APPEARANCE EVOKES IN PEOPLE TRULY INFURIATES ME ESPECIALLY BECAUSE, IN MANY WAYS, I AM A COWARD AND I AVOID CONFRONTATION AT ALL COSTS. ALSO, I AM ALWAYS THE OPPOSITE OF THE STEREOTYPES IMPOSED ON ME BY OTHERS.

THE STEREOTYPES PEOPLE HAVE OF ME ARE NUMEROUS AND I HAVE EXPERIENCED A VARIETY IN A NUMBER OF CONTEXTS:

A STREET THUG:

A MUSLIM TERRORIST:

AN UNEDUCATED IMMIGRANT:

OR A SEXUAL PERVERT WHO WANTS NOTHING MORE THAN TO MOLEST YOUR WHITE DAUGHTER:

WHEN I WAS IN HIGH SCHOOL AND COLLEGE MOST OF MY FRIENDS WERE WHITE. WHILE THEY WERE MOSTLY NICE PEOPLE, EVERY ONCE IN A WHILE I FELT UNEASE. FOR EXAMPLE I WAS REGULARLY ASKED:

WHERE ARE YOU FROM?

WHAT THEY USUALLY WANTED TO KNOW WAS MY NATIONALITY. I WOULD ONLY REPLY:

CHICAGO...

WHEN IT CAME TO GIRLS:

I KNOW A REALLY NICE GIRL YOU WOULD LIKE, SHE'S DARK LIKE YOU!!!

ONE OF MY FRIENDS, DAVE, WAS OPENLY RACIST TOWARDS EVERY NATIONALITY EXCEPT, CURIOUSLY, ARABS. I'M GUESSING THAT WAS ONLY WHEN I WAS AROUND.

SPICS, NIGGERS, CHINKS, HINDUS.

I WENT TO A FRAT PARTY ONCE AND THERE WAS ANOTHER DARK SKINNED GUY.

AS A JOKE, MY FRIEND JOHNNY SAID TO ME:

LOOK TOUFIC, A FRIEND OF YOURS...

78

THE FRIENDS I HUNG OUT WITH DURING COLLEGE WERE MOSTLY THE SAME FRIENDS I HAD IN HIGH SCHOOL AND I ALWAYS WANTED TO BREAK AWAY FROM THEM. I WANTED TO TRY TO BECOME MORE CULTURALLY AWARE AND HAVE DIVERSE FRIENDS BUT I NEVER COULD DO THAT.

WE WENT TO A COSTUME PARTY ONCE.

WE GENERALLY WENT OUT TO COLLEGE PARTIES AND GOT WASTED ON WEEKENDS.

AT THIS PARTICULAR PARTY THERE WAS A GUY DRESSED IN AN ARAB COSTUME.

I GUESS IT WOULDN'T HAVE BEEN SO BAD IF HE WASN'T SO RAMBUNCTIOUS AND LOUD.

I KEEL YOU!

I ALWAYS FELT LIKE A MASCOT OR THE TOKEN MINORITY IN THE ALL WHITE GROUP. I MEAN I ALWAYS STUCK OUT LIKE A SORE THUMB.

TOUFIC WILL DO IT - HE'LL DO ANYTHING!

I WAS SO INSECURE THAT I FELT THE NEED TO IMPRESS THEM BY BEHAVING WILDLY AND TAKING STUPID RISKS.

CHUG!! CHUG!! CHUG!! CHUG!! CHUG!

SOME GUY'S PARENTS WERE OUT OF TOWN ONCE AND A FRIEND AND I DECIDED TO RIP OFF THE PARENTS AS A PRANK.

WE STOLE SOME JEWELRY AND CASH, IT'S NOT THAT WE NEEDED MONEY, WE WERE JUST TRYING TO IMPRESS EVERYONE.

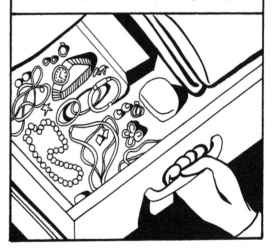

OF COURSE, WE WERE BUSTED AND I HAD TO TAKE ALL THE BLAME BECAUSE THE OTHER KID COPPED A DEAL TO TESTIFY AGAINST ME. EVENTUALLY I MATURED AND MOVED AWAY FROM THOSE FRIENDS.

GUILTY!!

IN COLLEGE I WANTED TO PROTEST AND EXPRESS SOLIDARITY WITH "MY PEOPLE." I BEGAN TO THINK THAT TRYING TO DENY MY NATIONALITY AND CULTURE WAS COWARDLY. BUT I WAS NO MUSLIM. RELIGION WAS JUST NOT SOMETHING I REALLY CARED ABOUT AND AGAIN, THE RESTRICTION ON VICES WAS ALWAYS THE MAJOR OBSTACLE. PART OF ME WAS ASHAMED FOR EMBRACING "AMERICAN DECADENT" CULTURE.

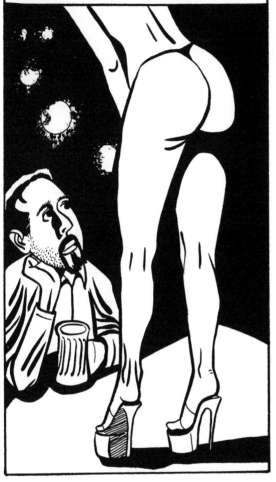

AND SO I WAS REJECTED BY MORE TRADITIONAL ARABS FOR BEING TOO AMERICANIZED. MY FATHER'S FRIEND INSISTED ON SPEAKING TO ME IN ARABIC

اَلْحَظْ لِلّهِ رَبِّ اَلْعَالَمِين

UHH, UHH, OKAY!

YOU DON'T EVEN SPEAK YOUR OWN LANGUAGE? YOU'RE NO ARAB!!

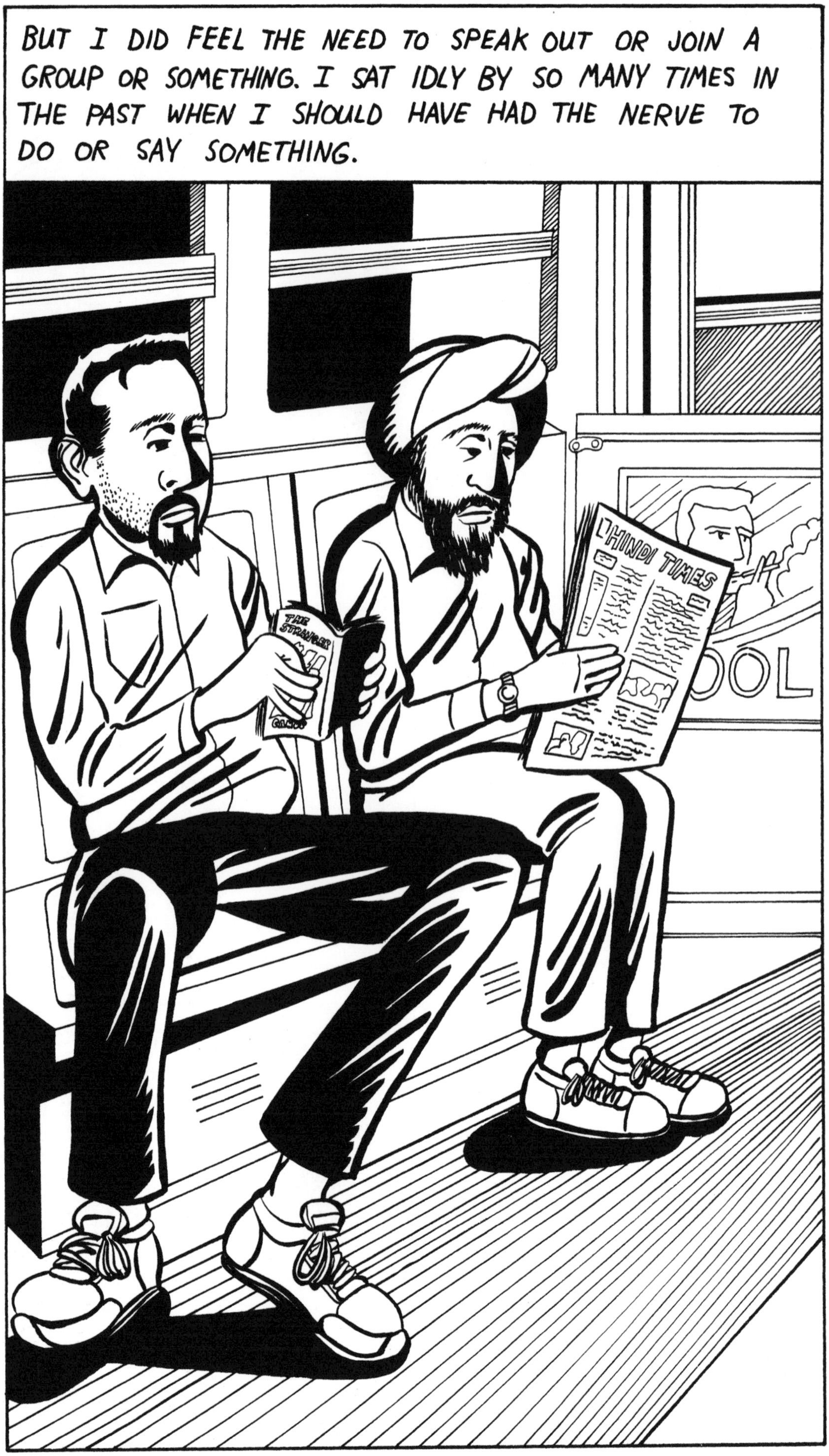
BUT I DID FEEL THE NEED TO SPEAK OUT OR JOIN A GROUP OR SOMETHING. I SAT IDLY BY SO MANY TIMES IN THE PAST WHEN I SHOULD HAVE HAD THE NERVE TO DO OR SAY SOMETHING.
THE STRANGER
HINDI TIMES
OOL

So I was like, yeah bitch!!

HA HA HA HA HA HA

So I was hell yeah beeotch!

HA HA HA HA

Hey, look at Osama over there.

I FELT LIKE I SHOULD SAY SOMETHING BUT I WAS SCARED. I WANTED TO TELL THEM THAT HE IS NOT EVEN ARAB. I WANTED TO STAND UP FOR HIM BUT FEAR HELD ME BACK. I WAS ASHAMED OF MYSELF AFTER THAT. I STILL AM.

IT REMINDED ME OF MY FATHER'S HUMILIATION WHEN I WAS YOUNGER. I GUESS EVERYONE REMEMBERS THE MOMENT WHEN HIS OR HER FATHER LOSES HIS AURA OF AUTHORITY. MY FATHER, BEING AN IMMIGRANT SPOKE WITH A THICK ACCENT. ONE DAY WE WERE SHOPPING.

WE GOT TO AN ELEVATOR AND WHEN THE DOORS OPENED A WORKER WITH SOME CRATES ASKED:

WHAT FLOOR?

I WANT TO FLOOR AHHH?

OH JESUS!

AFTER HE CLOSED THE DOOR ON US WE PRESSED THE BUTTON AGAIN AND WAITED.

THE DOORS OPENED AGAIN AND HE WAS STILL IN THE ELEVATOR.

YOU AGAIN? JESUS, WHY DON'T YOU LEARN ENGLISH?

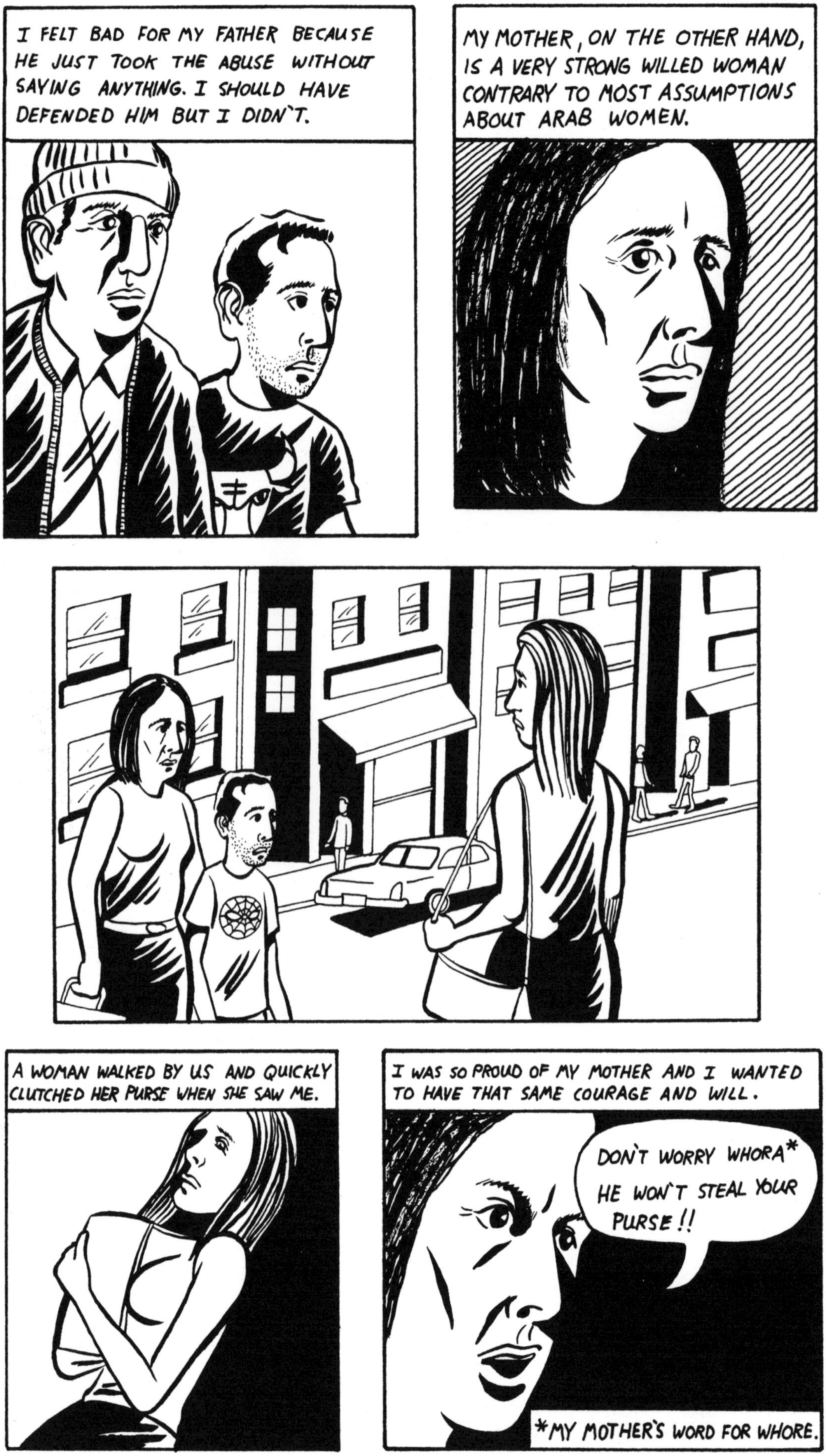
I FELT BAD FOR MY FATHER BECAUSE HE JUST TOOK THE ABUSE WITHOUT SAYING ANYTHING. I SHOULD HAVE DEFENDED HIM BUT I DIDN'T.
MY MOTHER, ON THE OTHER HAND, IS A VERY STRONG WILLED WOMAN CONTRARY TO MOST ASSUMPTIONS ABOUT ARAB WOMEN.
A WOMAN WALKED BY US AND QUICKLY CLUTCHED HER PURSE WHEN SHE SAW ME.
I WAS SO PROUD OF MY MOTHER AND I WANTED TO HAVE THAT SAME COURAGE AND WILL.
DON'T WORRY WHORA* HE WON'T STEAL YOUR PURSE!!
*MY MOTHER'S WORD FOR WHORE.

WITH THE DEFIANT EXAMPLE OF MY MOTHER IN MIND, I BECAME INCREASINGLY POLITICIZED AND RADICAL. I WAS INTRODUCED TO THE PUNK ROCK BAND "RAGE AGAINST THE MACHINE" IN HIGH SCHOOL BUT IT WASN'T UNTIL COLLEGE THAT I ACTUALLY LISTENED TO THEIR LYRICS.

THROUGH THE BAND I WAS INTRODUCED TO NOAM CHOMSKY:

FRANZ FANON.

CHE GUEVARA.

AND MAO TSE-TUNG.

IN RECENT YEARS COLLEGES AND UNIVERSITIES HAVE BEEN ATTACKED AS LIBERAL INSTITUTIONS DOMINATED BY RADICAL FACULTIES WHO TRY TO INDOCTRINATE THEIR STUDENTS. IN MY CASE MOST OF MY PROFESSORS WERE LIBERAL BUT BY NO MEANS WERE THEY RADICAL. IN FACT, SOME OF THEM WERE QUITE CONSERVATIVE.

THE MIDDLE EAST IS A CULTURAL WASTELAND FULL OF DICTATORS AND CHAINED TO AN ATAVISTIC RELIGION.

BUT AN ATMOSPHERE OF REBELLION AND EXPLORATION WAS PRESENT ON CAMPUS. ONE DAY I FOUND THE BOOK "KILLING HOPE" IN A BOX OUTSIDE OF THE BOOKSTORE.

WRITTEN BY FORMER STATE DEPARTMENT EMPLOYEE WILLIAM BLUM, IT CHARTS THE HISTORY OF U.S. MILITARY AND CIA INTERVENTIONS SINCE WORLD WAR 2. NEEDLESS TO SAY, IT HAD AN ENORMOUS IMPACT ON ME.

YEARS LATER, USAMA BIN LADEN'S RECOMMENDATION OF ANOTHER OF BLUM'S BOOKS, "ROGUE STATE" PROMPTED A BACKLASH AGAINST THE AUTHOR.

I TOOK A MARXIST PHILOSOPHY CLASS TAUGHT BY A MAOIST PROFESSOR THAT WAS ANOTHER BIG INFLUENCE.

WE LIVE IN A WORLD DOMINATED BY CAPITALISM AND IMPERIALISM!

I DEVOURED RADICAL LITERATURE AND THE CONCEPTS OF REBELLION AND ANTI-IMPERIALISM REALLY APPEALED TO ME. THEY FILLED A VOID IN ME, GAVE ME AN IDENTITY, AND PURPOSE. I NOW HAD A WAY OF UNDERSTANDING THE WORLD, AND ALL THE INJUSTICES THAT I SO VEHEMENTLY OPPOSED. THIS WAY OF THINKING EVENTUALLY OVERTOOK ME AND I DECLARED MYSELF A REVOLUTIONARY.

AND MY WARDROBE MADE THAT CLEAR:

I LEARNED TO SILK SCREEN SO I COULD MAKE MY OWN DESIGNS.

AT LAST I FOUND A CAUSE, AN IDENTITY, I NO LONGER HAD TO BE ASHAMED OF MY INACTION. ALL THE ALIENATION AND FRUSTRATION I FELT COULD NOW FIND EXPRESSION IN MY NEW RADICALISM BUT WHAT CAUSE WAS MOST IMPORTANT TO ME? IN COLLEGE THERE WAS A SMORGASBORD OF ORGANIZATIONS AND CAUSES TO JOIN, FROM OPPOSITION TO THE DEATH PENALTY TO ANIMAL RIGHTS TO ABORTION RIGHTS, IT WAS JUST A MATTER OF CHOOSING.

I GUESS I NEVER REALLY GRASPED WHAT IT MEANT TO BE A "REVOLUTIONARY" AND CLEARLY, I WAS OVERZEALOUS AND IMPRESSIONABLE BUT THESE RADICAL IDEAS DID HAVE A SIGNIFICANT INFLUENCE ON ME.

EVENTUALLY I WENT ON TO DEVELOP A MORE MATURE AND SOPHISTICATED APPROACH TOWARDS POLITICS AND PHILOSOPHY. I'M STILL TRYING TO NOT RETREAT COMPLETELY INTO CYNICISM.

BUT WHEN THE UNITED STATES INVADED AFGHANISTAN IN 2001 I WANTED TO BECOME INVOLVED IN THE PROTESTS AGAINST THE WAR. THE STUDENTS ON CAMPUS ORGANIZED AN ANTI WAR GROUP AND THAT IS WHEN STACY INVITED ME TO THEIR FIRST MEETING.

MOST OF THE STUDENT ACTIVISTS WERE WHITE AND CAME FROM MIDDLE CLASS FAMILIES AND I FELT UNCOMFORTABLE AROUND THEM BUT I DECIDED TO TRY TO GET INVOLVED ANY WAY.

BUT THERE WERE MANY OBSTACLES TO BECOMING INVOLVED IN THE ANTI-WAR MOVEMENT. MOST OF ALL, I WAS FEARFUL OF BEING ARRESTED OR DETAINED. FRIENDS OF MINE WHO WERE ACTIVE SEEMED TO FORGET ABOUT MY NATIONALITY AND IMMIGRATION STATUS.

HEY MAN, WE ARE GOING TO CHAIN OURSELVES TO THE DOORS OF THE FEDERAL BUILDING TO PROTEST — WANT TO JOIN US?

UMM... DON'T THINK SO.

ON THE FIRST ANNIVERSARY OF THE SEPTEMBER 11 ATTACKS, MY FRIENDS WANTED TO PASS OUT ANTI-WAR PROPAGANDA AT A VIGIL ON CAMPUS.

YOU WANT TO HELP PASS OUT FLYERS AT THE VIGIL?

IMAGES OF A MOB BEATING QUICKLY FILLED MY HEAD.

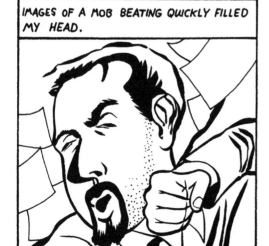

UMM... I DON'T THINK SO.

My Mexican friend Jorge, who was an activist, was a little more mindful of my dilemma. He told me of an experience he had once.

I DECIDED THE BEST THING TO DO WAS TO BECOME A U.S. CITIZEN. THE IMMIGRATION PROCESS IN THE U.S. IS NOT EXACTLY EASY TO NAVIGATE. MY DAD BECAME A CITIZEN BUT NOT MY MOM, SO THAT MEANT THAT I WASN'T A CITIZEN. EVEN THOUGH I SPENT ALMOST MY ENTIRE LIFE HERE, I WAS STILL SUBJECT TO DEPORTATION.

IF I FELT UNEASY BEING AN ARAB IN THE UNITED STATES BEFORE, IN THE POST 9/11 ATMOSPHERE IT WAS NERVE RACKING. ESPECIALLY SINCE I READ STORIES OF PEOPLE BEING DEPORTED TO THEIR BIRTH COUNTRIES AFTER SPENDING THEIR LIVES IN THE U.S.

LOEUN LUN CAME TO THE U.S. FROM CAMBODIA WITH HIS PARENTS WHEN HE WAS 6 YEARS OLD. THEY CAME AS REFUGEES, ESCAPING THE POLITICAL SITUATION WHICH BROUGHT THE KMHER ROUGE TO POWER. AS A TEENAGER LUN WAS CONVICTED OF ASSAULT AND SPENT 11 MONTHS IN JAIL. THAT WAS THE ONLY CRIME HE COMMITTED AND 9 YEARS LATER HE APPLIED FOR CITIZENSHIP WHICH BROUGHT HIM TO THE ATTENTION OF AUTHORITIES. IN HIS MID-20s, LUN WAS DEPORTED TO A COUNTRY HE DIDN'T KNOW, LEAVING HIS WIFE AND 2 KIDS BEHIND.

28 YEAR OLD BILL MUSTANICH WAS BORN IN EL SALVADOR BUT WAS ADOPTED BY AMERICAN PARENTS WHEN HE WAS 6 MONTHS OLD. HE WAS BROUGHT TO SAN JOSE WHERE HE GREW UP IN A MIDDLE CLASS NEIGHBORHOOD. WHEN HE WAS A TEENAGER HE WAS CONVICTED OF BURGLARIZING HIS FATHER'S HOUSE. IN 2005 HE WAS ORDERED DEPORTED BY AN IMMIGRATION JUDGE EVEN THOUGH HE SPENT HIS ENTIRE LIFE IN THE UNITED STATES; HE DOESN'T EVEN SPEAK SPANISH.

THE CASE OF THE KESBEHS IS ONE OF THE MOST INCREDIBLE EXAMPLES OF THE HEIGHTENED SCRUTINY ARABS FACE. THIS PALESTINIAN FAMILY WAS ONE OF MANY FAMILIES SWEPT UP IN THE POST 9/11 HYSTERIA, ESPECIALLY AFTER JOHN ASHCROFT LAUNCHED THE ABSCONDER APPREHENSION INITIATIVE INTENDED TO GO AFTER THE 314,000 IMMIGRANTS WHO WERE UNDER DEPORTATION ORDERS. THE VAST MAJORITY OF THE IMMIGRANTS ARE FROM LATIN AMERICA BUT THE JUSTICE DEPARTMENT FOCUSED ON THE 6,000 ARABS AND MUSLIMS. EVENTUALLY THE AUTHORITIES NOTICED THE KESBEH FAMILY.

AS A BOY, SHARIF (THE FATHER) FLED PALESTINE TO JORDAN AFTER ISRAEL WAS CREATED. HE GREW UP IN JORDAN BEFORE GOING TO SAUDI ARABIA WITH HIS FAMILY TO PURSUE A BUSINESS OPPORTUNITY. AFTER THE FIRST GULF WAR, THE FAMILY (LIKE MANY PALESTINIANS IN SAUDI ARABIA) SUFFERED PERSECUTION AND FLED TO THE U.S. WHERE THEY APPLIED FOR POLITICAL ASYLUM.

AFTER BUILDING A BUSINESS AND LIVING IN HOUSTON FOR 11 YEARS, THE KESBEHS WERE AN ORDINARY FAMILY, UNTIL MARCH 2002 WHEN 8 ARMED AGENTS BURST INTO THE FAMILY HOME AT DAWN AND ARRESTED SHARIF AND SON ALAA, LEAVING BEHIND THE MOTHER AND OTHER 5 CHILDREN.

DESPITE INTERVENTION BY VARIOUS CONGRESSMEN AND OTHERS, THE ENTIRE KESBEH FAMILY WAS PUT ON A PLANE TO JORDAN. THE FAMILY NOW LIVES IN A REFUGEE CAMP IN AMMAN AND BECAUSE THE U.S. IMMIGRATION OFFICIALS CONFISCATED THEIR JORDANIAN PASSPORTS, THE FAMILY IS ESSENTIALLY STUCK THERE.

THE CHILDREN, WHO HAVE NEVER BEEN TO JORDAN AND BARELY SPEAK ARABIC (ALL OF THEM ARE MORE AMERICAN THAN ARAB) HAVE TO ADJUST TO THIS COMPLETELY NEW ENVIRONMENT WITHOUT THE POSSIBILITY OF RETURNING.

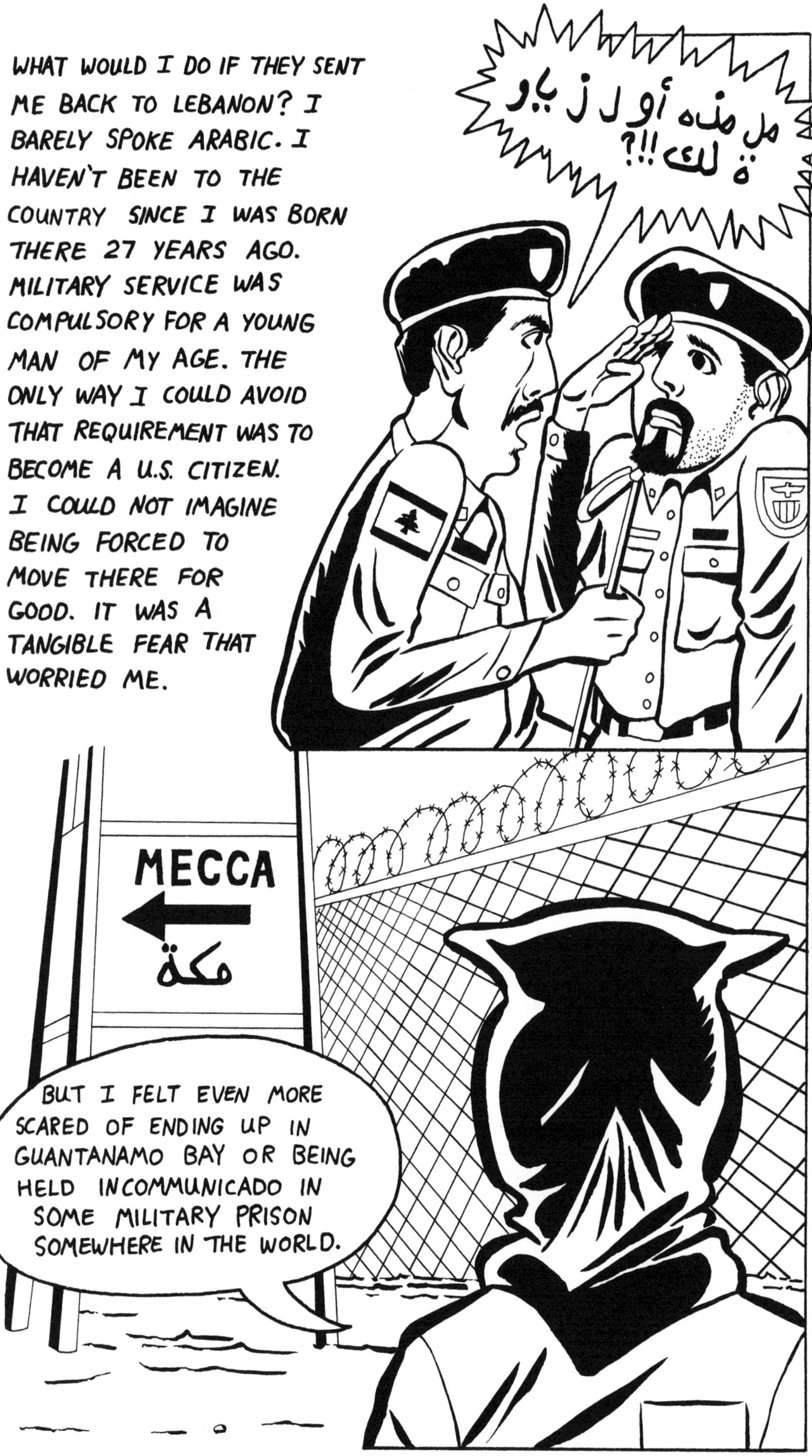
WHAT WOULD I DO IF THEY SENT ME BACK TO LEBANON? I BARELY SPOKE ARABIC. I HAVEN'T BEEN TO THE COUNTRY SINCE I WAS BORN THERE 27 YEARS AGO. MILITARY SERVICE WAS COMPULSORY FOR A YOUNG MAN OF MY AGE. THE ONLY WAY I COULD AVOID THAT REQUIREMENT WAS TO BECOME A U.S. CITIZEN. I COULD NOT IMAGINE BEING FORCED TO MOVE THERE FOR GOOD. IT WAS A TANGIBLE FEAR THAT WORRIED ME.
MECCA
مكة
BUT I FELT EVEN MORE SCARED OF ENDING UP IN GUANTANAMO BAY OR BEING HELD INCOMMUNICADO IN SOME MILITARY PRISON SOMEWHERE IN THE WORLD.

A FEW CASES INVOLVING AMERICAN DETAINEES REALLY STOKED MY FEARS. FOR EXAMPLE, THE NORTHERN ALLIANCE CAPTURED YASSER HAMDI IN AFGHANISTAN DURING THE U.S. INVASION IN 2001. HAMDI IS SAUDI ARABIAN AND THE U.S. CLAIMED HE WAS IN AFGHANISTAN FIGHTING ON BEHALF OF THE TALIBAN. HAMDI (THROUGH HIS FATHER) DENIED HE WAS A FIGHTER, CLAIMING HE WAS IN AFGHANISTAN DOING HUMANITARIAN RELIEF WORK.

INITIALLY HELD IN GUANTANAMO BAY, IT WAS DISCOVERED THAT HAMDI HELD U.S. CITIZENSHIP HAVING BEEN BORN IN LOUISIANA. ONCE THAT WAS REVEALED, HE WAS TRANSFERRED OUT OF GUANTANAMO AND SENT TO A NAVAL BRIG IN NORFOLK, VIRGINIA AND LATER TO CHARLESTON, SOUTH CAROLINA.

THE BUSH ADMINISTRATION ARGUED THAT HAMDI COULD BE HELD AS AN "UNLAWFUL ENEMY COMBATANT" WITHOUT ACCESS TO A LAWYER OR THE COURT SYSTEM.

IN 2002 HIS FATHER FILED A HABEAS PETITION IN VIRGINIA, AND HAMDI'S CASE ENDED UP IN THE U.S. SUPREME COURT. THE COURT FOUND THAT THE PRESIDENT DOES NOT HAVE THE POWER TO HOLD A U.S. CITIZEN INDEFINITELY.

IN 2004, AFTER ABOUT 3 YEARS IN JAIL, WITHOUT CHARGES, HAMDI WAS FREED. HOWEVER, BEFORE HIS RELEASE, HAMDI HAD TO AGREE TO BE RELEASED TO SAUDI ARABIA (WHERE HE ALSO HAS CITIZENSHIP) AND AGREE TO GIVE UP HIS U.S. CITIZENSHIP, AND AGREE TO NEVER GO TO AFGHANISTAN, IRAQ, ISRAEL, PAKISTAN, SYRIA, OR BACK TO THE UNITED STATES.

JOSE PADILLA (AKA ABDULLAH AL MUHAJIR) IS A U.S. BORN AMERICAN CITIZEN OF PUERTO RICAN DECENT. HE HAD A TROUBLED YOUTH GROWING UP IN CHICAGO BUT LATER, HE CONVERTED TO ISLAM. IN 2002 HE TRAVELED TO THE MIDDLE EAST AND WHEN HE RETURNED TO THE U.S. HE WAS ARRESTED AT CHICAGO'S O'HARE AIRPORT.

HE WAS ACCUSED OF PLOTTING WITH AL QAEDA TO BLOW UP A "DIRTY BOMB" IN THE U.S. HE WAS LABELED AN "ILLEGAL ENEMY COMBATANT" BY THE GOVERNMENT, THEREFORE NOT PROTECTED BY U.S. LAW OR THE GENEVA CONVENTIONS. IT WAS NOT UNTIL 2005 THAT HE WAS CHARGED WITH "CONSPIRACY TO MURDER, KIDNAP AND MAIM OVERSEAS." HE HAS BEEN IN DETENTION FOR MORE THAN 4 YEARS.

BOTH HAMDI AND PADILLA ARE U.S. CITIZENS. I WAS JUST A PERMANENT RESIDENT, WHICH MEANT THAT I HAD CONSIDERABLY FEWER RIGHTS THAN AN AMERICAN CITIZEN.

98

UNLIKE THE PADILLA AND HAMDI CASES, THE CASE OF MAHER ARAR, A 34 YEAR OLD SYRIAN BORN MAN WHO BECAME A CANADIAN CITIZEN, IS ESPECIALLY DISTRESSING BECAUSE THERE IS ABSOLUTELY NO EVIDENCE THAT HE WAS EVER INVOLVED IN TERRORISM AND YET HE WAS DEPORTED TO SYRIA WHERE HE ENDURED 10 MONTHS OF TORTURE.

AFTER EARNING A MASTERS DEGREE, ARAR BECAME A WIRELESS TECHNOLOGY CONSULTANT. BY ALL ACCOUNTS HE WAS A FAMILY MAN WHO HAD 2 CHILDREN WITH HIS WIFE MONIA. THEY SEEMED TO LIVE A NORMAL LIFE IN OTTAWA UNTIL SEPTEMBER 2002.

ARAR AND HIS FAMILY WERE ON VACATION IN TUNISIA WHEN HE HAD TO RETURN TO CANADA BEFORE HIS FAMILY FOR WORK. ON HIS WAY BACK, ARAR'S PLANE STOPPED OVER AT JFK AIRPORT IN NEW YORK WHERE HE WAS DETAINED BY U.S. OFFICIALS AND INTERROGATED ABOUT AN ALLEGED CONNECTION WITH AL QAEDA. AFTER 12 DAYS IN CUSTODY, HE WAS FLOWN IN A PRIVATE JET TO JORDAN AND THEN, BLINDFOLDED, HE WAS DRIVEN TO SYRIA WHERE HE WAS PUT IN PRISON.

OVER THE NEXT 10 MONTHS ARAR WAS HELD IN A TINY CELL WITH NO LIGHT AND SUBJECTED TO INTERROGATION, BEATING, AND TORTURE. HIS TORMENTORS DEMANDED THAT HE ADMIT TO BEING ASSOCIATED WITH AL QAEDA AND CONFESS TO VISITING AFGHANISTAN. EVENTUALLY, HE MADE A FALSE CONFESSION. DURING HIS IMPRISIONMENT, ARAR'S WIFE CAMPAIGNED RELENTLESSLY ON HIS BEHALF AND EVENTUALLY HE WAS FREED.

U.S. OFFICIALS INSIST HE IS GUILTY OF SOME SORT OF TERRORIST ACTIVITY BUT THEY REFUSE TO REVEAL ANY PROOF. ARAR HAS NEVER BEEN CHARGED WITH A CRIME AND HE'S FREE IN CANADA TODAY.

ARAR'S CASE HIGHLIGHTS THE PRACTICE OF "RENDITION," IN WHICH THE U.S. SENDS TERROR SUSPECTS TO OTHER COUNTRIES FOR QUESTIONING. SINCE 9/11 IT IS BELIEVED THAT THE U.S. HAS SENT HUNDREDS OF PEOPLE TO THE MIDDLE EAST FOR INTERROGATIONS.

WHEN I APPLIED FOR CITIZENSHIP, I DIDN'T HAVE MONEY FOR A LAWYER. I THOUGHT THAT I WASN'T A "REAL" IMMIGRANT, I WAS PRACTICALLY AMERICAN, I COULD FIGURE THIS OUT RIGHT? I WAS WRONG.

I HAD SOME QUESTIONS, SO I WENT DOWN TO IMMIGRATION AND NATURALIZATION SERVICES. THIS WAS BEFORE THEY MADE IT PART OF HOMELAND SECURITY. IT TURNS OUT THAT MANY PEOPLE HAVE QUESTIONS ABOUT IMMIGRATION.

I STOOD IN LINE FOR 3 HOURS WHEN AN OFFICIAL CAME DOWN THE LINE HANDING OUT WHAT LOOKED LIKE RAFFLE TICKETS.

OF COURSE SHE STOPPED AT THE PERSON RIGHT BEFORE ME, THEN TURNED AND WALKED AWAY. EVERYONE BEHIND ME JUST LEFT AND WHEN I TRIED TO ASK A QUESTION, SHE JUST KEPT WALKING.

THE NEXT DAY, I DECIDED TO SHOW UP EARLIER. THE DOORS OPENED AT 7 AM SO I THOUGHT IT WAS A GOOD IDEA TO GET THERE AT 6 AM. SO DID MANY OTHERS.

I QUICKLY LEARNED THAT I WAS NO DIFFERENT THAN ALL THE OTHER IMMIGRANTS STANDING IN THAT LINE. IT DIDN'T MATTER IF YOU LIVED HERE FOR 30 YEARS OR 3 YEARS, YOU WERE TREATED LIKE SHIT BECAUSE YOU WERE NOT A CITIZEN.

KEEP THE LINE MOVIN'! MOVE IT! MOVE IT!

I COULDN'T TELL YOU HOW MANY TIMES I WAS ASKED IF I SPOKE ENGLISH. MOST OF THE TIME THEY WOULD ASK BEFORE THEY EVEN LOOKED AT ME.

DO YOU SPEAK ENGLISH?

ONCE, I ACTUALLY SPOKE BEFORE I COULD BE ASKED BUT I WAS ASKED ANYWAY!

HI, I HAVE A QUESTION.

DO YOU SPEAK ENGLISH?

SO I FELT DEEPLY INSULTED BUT IT WAS A REMINDER THAT I WASN'T WHITE, SO I SHOULD NOT BE SO SURPRISED. IT WAS A LESSON LEARNED — THAT THIS IS NOT MY COUNTRY, AND NEVER COULD BE.

THAT'S THE WAY IT WENT, I THOUGHT I COULD GET HELP BUT I WAS ON MY OWN WITH THESE PEOPLE. IT WAS LIKE GOING TO THE DMV BUT YOU COULD GET DEPORTED IF THEY DON'T LIKE YOU.

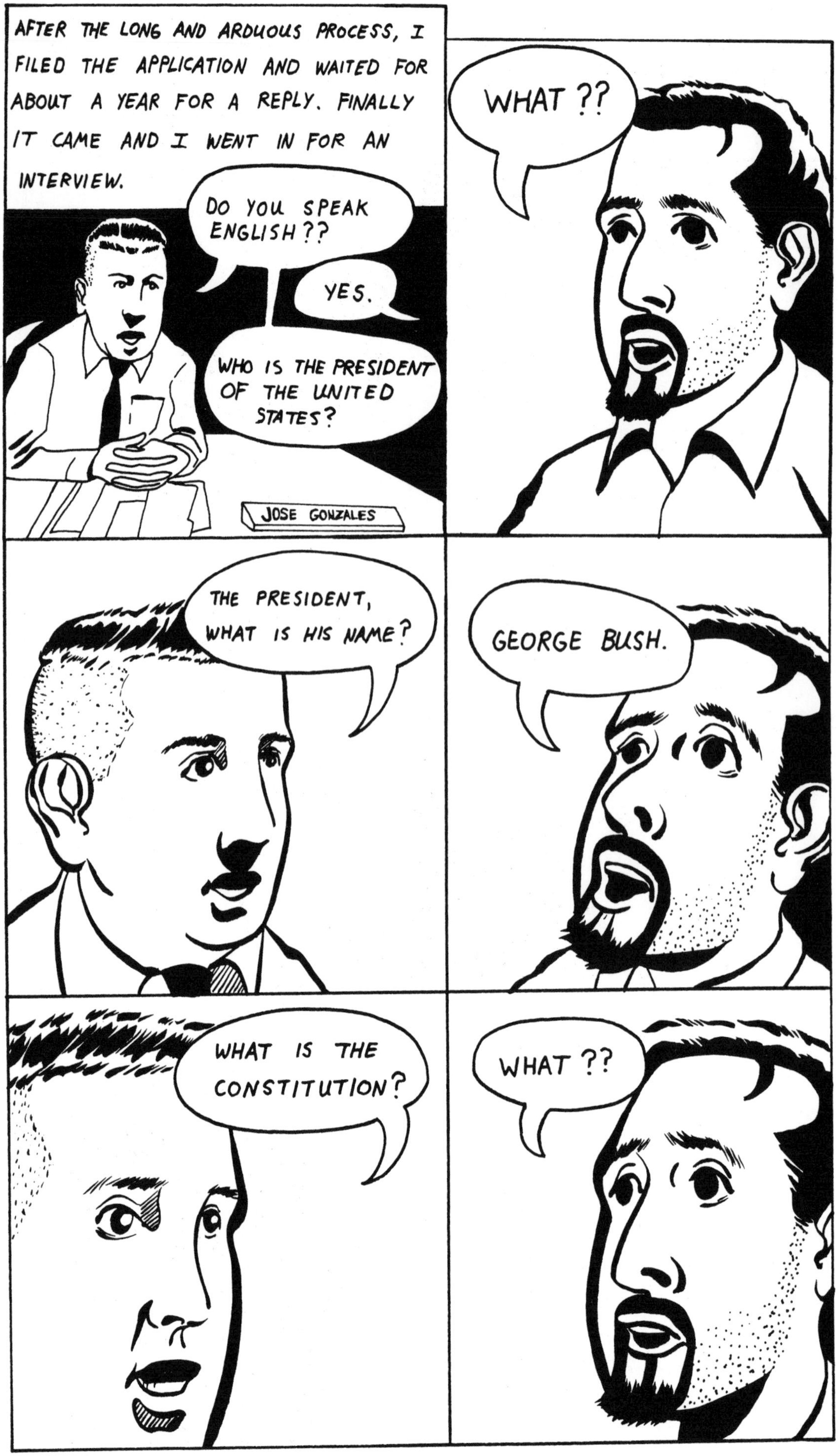
AFTER THE LONG AND ARDUOUS PROCESS, I FILED THE APPLICATION AND WAITED FOR ABOUT A YEAR FOR A REPLY. FINALLY IT CAME AND I WENT IN FOR AN INTERVIEW.
DO YOU SPEAK ENGLISH??
YES.
WHO IS THE PRESIDENT OF THE UNITED STATES?
JOSE GONZALES
WHAT??
THE PRESIDENT, WHAT IS HIS NAME?
GEORGE BUSH.
WHAT IS THE CONSTITUTION?
WHAT??

IT WENT ON LIKE THAT FOR A FEW MINUTES, THEN HE SAID:

OK, EVERYTHING SEEMS IN ORDER HERE BUT I CAN'T GIVE YOU AN ANSWER RIGHT NOW, SO YOU WILL GET ONE IN THE MAIL.

WHY CAN'T YOU GIVE ME AN ANSWER NOW?

WELL, IT NEEDS TO GET APPROVED BY THE HIGHER UPS.

USUALLY THEY GIVE YOU AN ANSWER ON THE SPOT, SO I HAD NO IDEA WHAT HE MEANT. BUT I FIGURED THAT IT IS BETTER TO KEEP MY MOUTH SHUT THAN RISK PISSING HIM OFF, SO I SAID:

RIGHT, RIGHT I SEE...

AFTER A FEW MORE MONTHS OF WAITING, I FINALLY RECEIVED A LETTER IN THE MAIL INSTRUCTING ME TO GO DOWNTOWN TO THE FEDERAL BUILDING TO SWEAR AN OATH, THUS OFFICIALLY BECOMING A UNITED STATES CITIZEN.

THE CEREMONY TOOK PLACE IN A FEDERAL DISTRICT COURTROOM. THERE WERE ABOUT 300 OTHER PEOPLE THERE, MANY OF THEM DRESSED IN THEIR BEST; IT WAS LIKE THEY WERE GOING TO A WEDDING OR SOMETHING. SOME PEOPLE HAD FAMILY MEMBERS THERE TAKING PICTURES FROM THE SIDE OF THE ROOM. I NEVER SAW SUCH HAPPINESS. I GUESS I SHOULD HAVE BEEN HAPPIER.

THE JUDGE CAME IN AND WE ALL HAD TO STAND UP, LIKE ON TELEVISION. THE ATMOSPHERE WAS BIZARRE, BEFORE HE GAVE US THE OATH HE GAVE THIS SPEECH THAT WAS SUPPOSE TO INSPIRE US OR SOMETHING.

MY GRANDPARENTS ARRIVED HERE FROM CZECHOSLOVAKIA 60 YEARS AGO WITH ONLY A FEW DOLLARS IN THEIR POCKET.

AFTER I BECAME A CITIZEN, I FELT A LITTLE SAFER AND SO IN MARCH OF 2003, WHEN THE UNITED STATES INVADED IRAQ, IN THE FACE OF INTERNATIONAL OPPOSITION, I PROTESTED LIKE MANY OTHERS ACROSS THE GLOBE.

AFTER MORE THAN 10 YEARS OF SANCTIONS AND BOMBARDMENT, THE BUSH REGIME DECIDED THAT IT WAS TIME TO INVADE IRAQ AND REMOVE SADDAM HUSSEIN FROM POWER. THE IRONY IS THAT HUSSEIN WAS A VERY CLOSE ALLY OF THE UNITED STATES DURING THE 1980s AND WAS FULLY SUPPORTED BY THE REAGAN ADMINISTRATION. AFTER SADDAM'S 1990 INVASION OF KUWAIT HOWEVER, THE RELATIONSHIP FRACTURED AND THE UNITED STATES LED THE WAY TO WAR IN 1991.

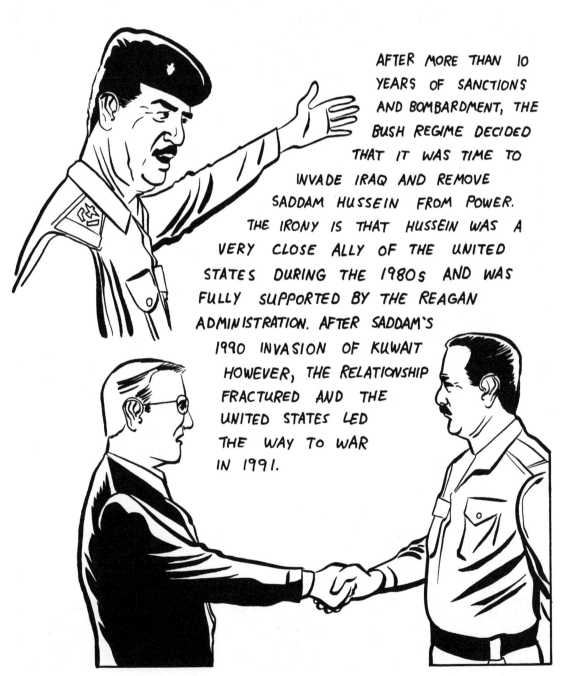

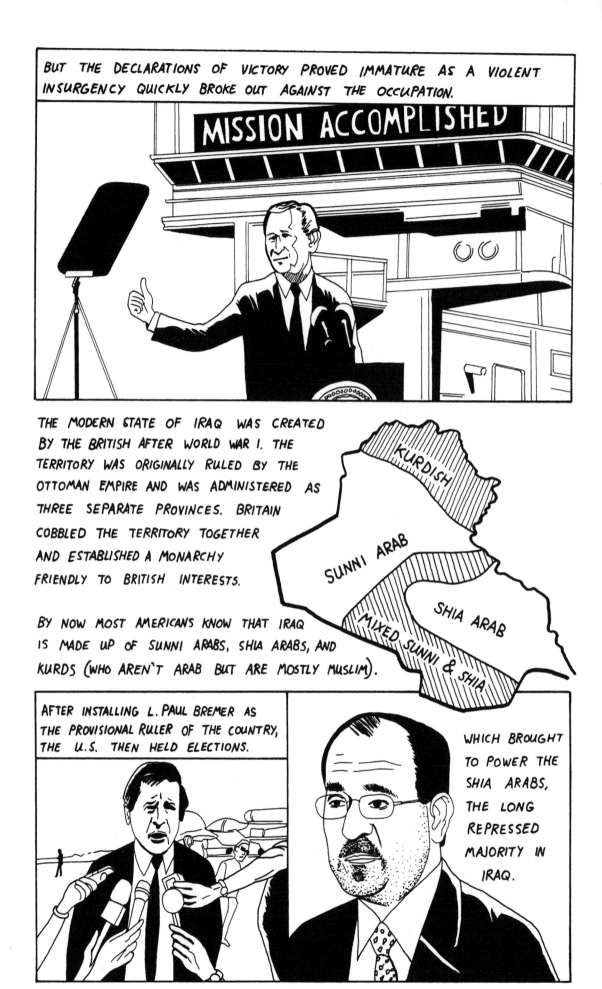

BUT THE DECLARATIONS OF VICTORY PROVED IMMATURE AS A VIOLENT INSURGENCY QUICKLY BROKE OUT AGAINST THE OCCUPATION.

MISSION ACCOMPLISHED

THE MODERN STATE OF IRAQ WAS CREATED BY THE BRITISH AFTER WORLD WAR I. THE TERRITORY WAS ORIGINALLY RULED BY THE OTTOMAN EMPIRE AND WAS ADMINISTERED AS THREE SEPARATE PROVINCES. BRITAIN COBBLED THE TERRITORY TOGETHER AND ESTABLISHED A MONARCHY FRIENDLY TO BRITISH INTERESTS.

KURDISH

SUNNI ARAB

SHIA ARAB

MIXED SUNNI & SHIA

BY NOW MOST AMERICANS KNOW THAT IRAQ IS MADE UP OF SUNNI ARABS, SHIA ARABS, AND KURDS (WHO AREN'T ARAB BUT ARE MOSTLY MUSLIM).

AFTER INSTALLING L. PAUL BREMER AS THE PROVISIONAL RULER OF THE COUNTRY, THE U.S. THEN HELD ELECTIONS.

WHICH BROUGHT TO POWER THE SHIA ARABS, THE LONG REPRESSED MAJORITY IN IRAQ.

WITH THE RISE OF THE SO-CALLED NEOCONSERVATIVES, THE PLAN TO INVADE AND "REMAKE" THE MIDDLE EAST BY SPREADING "DEMOCRACY" HAD BEEN IN THE WORKS FOR MANY YEARS.

AFTER THE SEPTEMBER 11 ATTACKS AND WITH BUSH IN THE WHITE HOUSE, THE WAR SEEMED INEVITABLE.

THE INVASION ITSELF WAS EASY ENOUGH, AFTER ALL, THE IRAQI ARMY WAS DECIMATED AFTER THE FIRST GULF WAR AND THE COUNTRY WAS IN SHAMBLES AFTER THE SANCTIONS PREVENTED ANY KIND OF RECOVERY.

THE INSURGENCY AGAINST THE OCCUPATION IS NOW COUPLED WITH AN INCREASINGLY VIOLENT CIVIL WAR, WITH EACH OF THE COUNTRY'S FACTIONS STRUGGLING FOR POWER IN THIS NEW IRAQ.

AS THE VIOLENCE SPIRALS OUT OF CONTROL, THE U.S. AND BRITISH SOLDIERS CONTINUE TO OCCUPY THE COUNTRY RESULTING IN THOUSANDS OF DEATHS AND MUCH DESTRUCTION WITH NO END IN SIGHT.

FOR SOME REASON, I CAME TO BELIEVE THAT LIBERAL PEOPLE WOULD BE MORE SYMPATHETIC AND TOLERANT BUT I WAS WRONG. I LEARNED VALUABLE LESSONS BEING AROUND "PROGRESSIVE" PEOPLE.

FOR ONE THING, I LEARNED THAT CONDESCENDING PEOPLE COME IN ALL SHAPES AND SIZES, REGARDLESS OF POLITICAL ORIENTATION. MOST OF THE PEOPLE IN THE ANTI-WAR MOVEMENT ARE WHITE, AND AT A FEW MEETINGS A SENTIMENT WAS EXPRESSED:

I THINK WE NEED MORE PEOPLE OF COLOR...

SOMETIMES I WAS THE ONLY "PERSON OF COLOR" IN THE MEETING BUT I WAS IGNORED WHILE OTHERS SPOKE WITH AUTHORITY ON WHAT "PEOPLE OF COLOR" NEED.

PEOPLE OF COLOR NEED JOBS!

OTHER TIMES, I WOULD OFFER AN OPINION BUT THAT USUALLY RESULTED IN AN AWKWARD IMPASSE DURING THE MEETING.

I THINK WE SHOULD SUPPORT THE PALESTINIANS

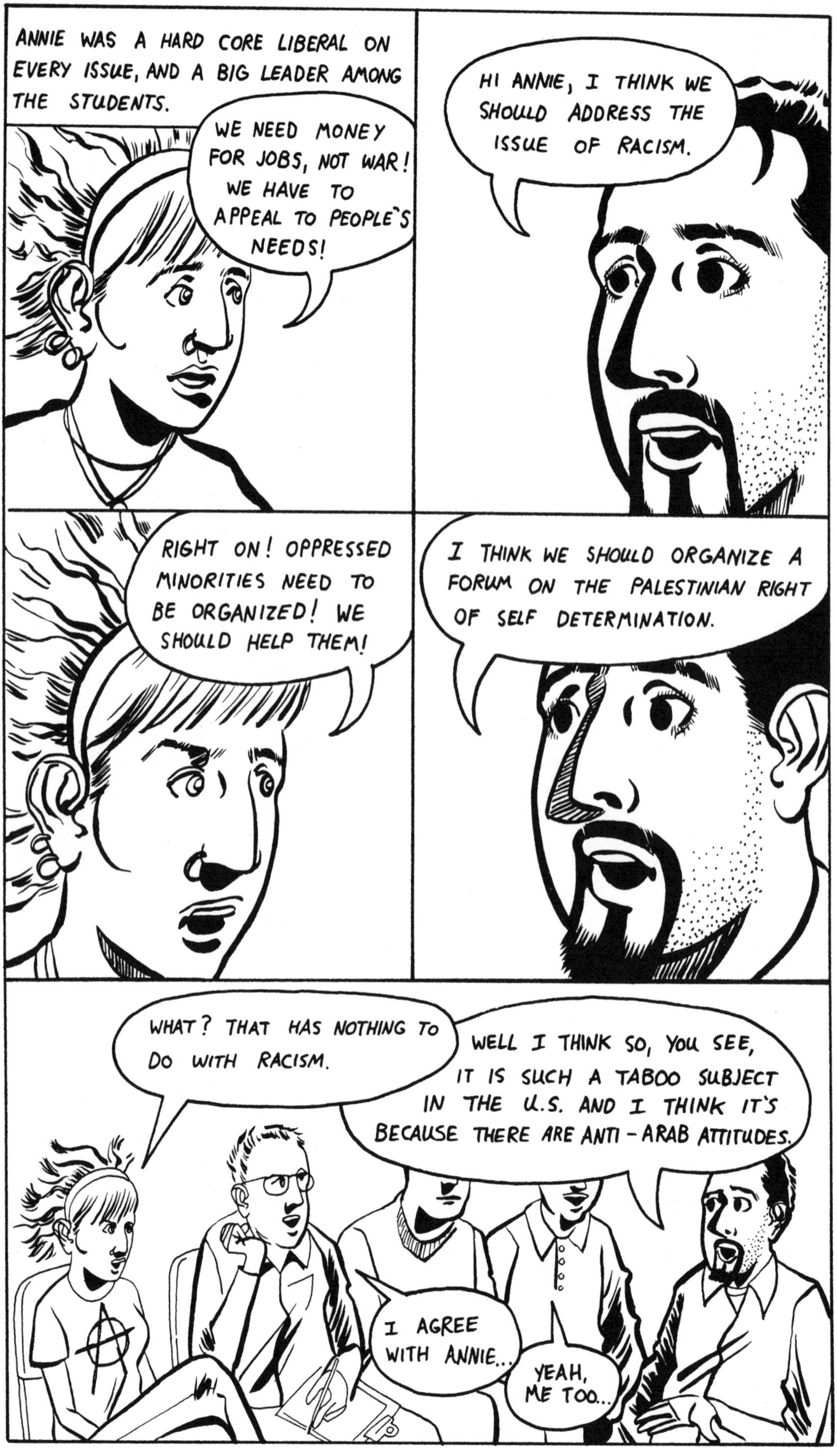
ANNIE WAS A HARD CORE LIBERAL ON EVERY ISSUE, AND A BIG LEADER AMONG THE STUDENTS.
WE NEED MONEY FOR JOBS, NOT WAR! WE HAVE TO APPEAL TO PEOPLE'S NEEDS!
HI ANNIE, I THINK WE SHOULD ADDRESS THE ISSUE OF RACISM.
RIGHT ON! OPPRESSED MINORITIES NEED TO BE ORGANIZED! WE SHOULD HELP THEM!
I THINK WE SHOULD ORGANIZE A FORUM ON THE PALESTINIAN RIGHT OF SELF DETERMINATION.
WHAT? THAT HAS NOTHING TO DO WITH RACISM.
WELL I THINK SO, YOU SEE, IT IS SUCH A TABOO SUBJECT IN THE U.S. AND I THINK IT'S BECAUSE THERE ARE ANTI-ARAB ATTITUDES.
I AGREE WITH ANNIE...
YEAH, ME TOO...

BESIDES, IF ANYTHING, THERE IS ANTI-SEMITISM AGAINST JEWS. THE ISRAELIS HAVE A RIGHT TO EXIST!

IT SEEMED TO ME THAT EVEN AMONG THE LEFT, I WAS STILL AN OUTSIDER.

I SEE...

THE FUNNY THING IS THAT I FELT MORE HOSTILITY FROM LIBERALS THAN FROM CONSERVATIVES. I THINK IT IS BECAUSE I ALWAYS KNEW WHERE I STOOD WITH RIGHT WING PEOPLE:

I DON'T SUPPORT YOU. GO BACK TO YOUR COUNTRY PAKI.

NEVER FORGET

LIBERAL PEOPLE ARE NOT AS FORTHRIGHT ABOUT THEIR FEELINGS.

HEY TOUFIC, MAYBE YOU SHOULDN'T SPEAK AT THIS EVENT. YOU KNOW, WE DON'T WANT TO SCARE PEOPLE.

I'LL NEVER FORGET WHEN I WENT TO A PHOTO EXHIBIT CALLED "IMAGES OF PALESTINE" WHICH WAS A SHOW OF PHOTOGRAPHS TAKEN BY MATT, A YOUNG, WHITE, COLLEGE STUDENT, WHO TRAVELED TO THE WEST BANK AND THE GAZA STRIP.

THE PICTURES WERE MOSTLY OF DESTITUTE CHILDREN STANDING BAREFOOT IN MUD AND SURROUNDED BY DEVASTATION. THERE WERE ALSO PHOTOS OF ORDINARY PALESTINIANS JUST SITTING AT A TABLE, IT SEEMED EXPLOITATIVE IN SOME WAY.

IT OCCURRED TO ME THAT EVERYTHING THAT AMERICANS KNOW ABOUT ARABS IS ALMOST ALWAYS FILTERED THROUGH THE EYES OF A WHITE AMERICAN, NO MATTER HIS/HER POLITICAL PHILOSOPHY. WHETHER IT WAS A PUGNACIOUS COMMENTATOR PONTIFICATING ON THE "ARAB MIND" OR A WELL MEANING COLLEGE STUDENT, ARABS ARE ALWAYS REPRESENTED BY SOMEONE ELSE.

I FELT LIKE I HAD NO VOICE TO SPEAK FOR MYSELF, INSTEAD I HAD TO LISTEN WHILE OTHERS SPOKE FOR ME AND IT WAS ALWAYS PEOPLE WHO DIDN'T KNOW WHAT THEY WERE TALKING ABOUT.

BEING IN AMERICA MEANS LIVING IN A SOCIETY BUT NOT BEING PART OF IT. AN ARAB HAS 2 CHOICES, EITHER BE CONSTANTLY ON THE DEFENSIVE, OR HIDE YOUR IDENTITY.

AFTER YEARS OF BEING ASHAMED OF WHO I AM, HAVING AN "AMERICAN" NAME, OBSCURING MY ETHNICITY, I BEGAN TO REALIZE THAT I HAD NO REASON TO BE ASHAMED. IN FACT, AFTER LEARNING THE HISTORY OF MY PEOPLE AND UNDERSTANDING MY CULTURE MORE, I BECAME PROUD OF MY NATIONALITY.

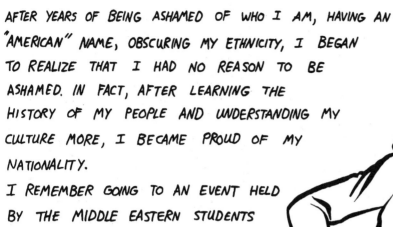

I REMEMBER GOING TO AN EVENT HELD BY THE MIDDLE EASTERN STUDENTS ASSOCIATION AT MY SCHOOL. THERE WAS A MUSICIAN PLAYING CLASSICAL ARAB SONGS AS PEOPLE MINGLED DURING THE PERFORMANCE. AS THE MUSIC FILLED THE ROOM, I NOTICED THE BEAUTY OF THE PEOPLE AROUND ME.

LONG EYELASHES AND THICK, FULL EYEBROWS.

BIG, ROUND, PIERCING, DARK, EYES.

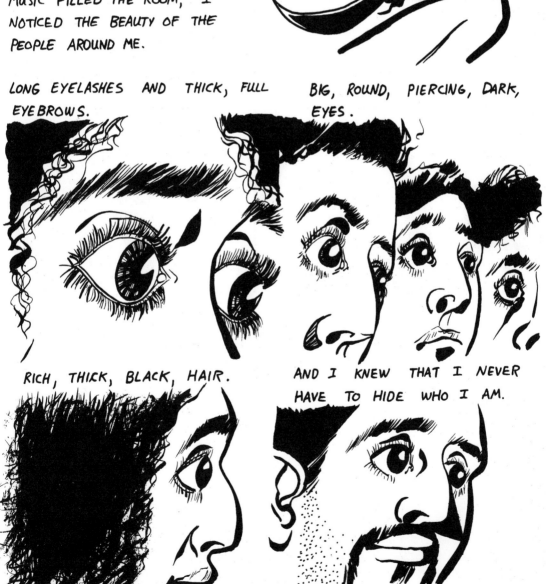

RICH, THICK, BLACK, HAIR.

AND I KNEW THAT I NEVER HAVE TO HIDE WHO I AM.

WITH MY NEWFOUND PRIDE, I DECIDED TO VISIT LEBANON AND SEE THE COUNTRY WHERE I WAS BORN. BUT THERE WAS ONE BIG OBSTACLE, I HAD TO GO TO THE AIRPORT, WHICH I STEADFASTLY AVOIDED SINCE 9/11.

THERE HAVE BEEN A NUMBER OF INCIDENTS IN WHICH ARABS OR THOSE UNFORTUNATE ENOUGH TO BE CONFUSED AS ARAB, HAVE BEEN DETAINED OR EXPELLED FROM FLIGHTS SINCE 2001.

I.D. PLEASE.

IN DECEMBER OF 2001, WALID SHATER, A SECRET SERVICE AGENT OF ARAB DESCENT, WAS EXPELLED FROM A FLIGHT TO TEXAS WHERE HE WAS TO JOIN THE SECURITY DETAIL AT THE PRESIDENT'S RANCH.

ONE OF THE SUSPICIOUS FLIGHT ATTENDANTS NOTICED SHATER WITH BOOKS, "WHICH WERE WRITTEN IN WHAT SHE ASSESSED WAS ARABIC-STYLE PRINT."

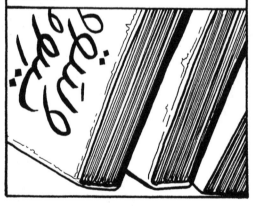

THE THREATENING TEXT IN QUESTION TURNED OUT TO BE A COPY OF A GREAT BOOK, "THE CRUSADES THROUGH ARAB EYES" BY AMIN MAALOUF.

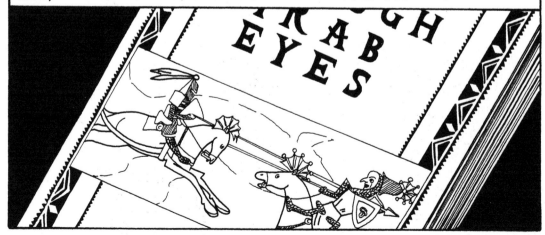

IN AUGUST OF 2006, RAED JARAR, AN ARAB-AMERICAN, WAS FORCED OFF A JET BLUE FLIGHT IN NEW YORK'S JFK AIRPORT, AND MADE TO TAKE OFF HIS T-SHIRT BECAUSE IT HAD ARABIC WRITING ON IT. IT WAS ALSO SAID TO BE "MAKING OTHER PASSENGERS UNCOMFORTABLE." I NEVER REALIZED HOW OFFENSIVE THE ARABIC SCRIPT COULD BE TO SOME PEOPLE.

THE BLACK COTTON T-SHIRT BORE THE SLOGAN, "WE WILL NOT BE SILENT," IN BOTH ARABIC AND ENGLISH. THE PHRASE WAS ADOPTED BY OPPONENTS OF THE WAR IN IRAQ AND OTHER CONFLICTS IN THE MIDDLE EAST. IT IS DERIVED FROM THE WHITE ROSE DISSIDENT GROUP WHICH OPPOSED THE NAZIS IN GERMANY MANY YEARS AGO.

I DECIDED TO PLAY IT SAFE AT THE AIRPORT.

I'VE LIVED HERE MY WHOLE LIFE AND AFTER ALL THESE YEARS I STILL FEEL LIKE AN OUTSIDER. WHO KNOWS, MAYBE LEBANON WILL BE DIFFERENT.

NOW BOARDING...

WHO KNOWS, MAYBE I'LL STAY...

THE END.

EPILOGUE

IN JULY 2006, 2 ISRAELI SOLDIERS WERE CAPTURED BY HEZBOLLAH, A SHIA MILITIA THAT HAS MUCH INFLUENCE IN LEBANON BECAUSE 60 PERCENT OF THE COUNTRY'S POPULATION ARE SHIA WHO ARE DENIED POLITICAL POWER COMMENSURATE WITH THEIR NUMBERS.

EHUD OLMERT, THE PRIME MINISTER OF ISRAEL, WHO TOOK POWER AFTER FORMER PRIME MINISTER ARIEL SHARON'S STROKE, ORDERED THE BOMBING AND INVASION OF LEBANON AFTER THE CAPTURE OF THE ISRAELI SOLDIERS.

ISRAEL TARGETED CIVILIAN INFRASTRUCTURE IN LEBANON, DESTROYING FACTORIES, ROADS, AND MORE THAN 90 PERCENT OF ALL BRIDGES. THE BOMBING LASTED FOR 5 WEEKS AND COMPLETELY DESTROYED MUCH OF THE RECONSTRUCTION OF LEBANON SINCE THE CIVIL WAR, SETTING IT BACK MANY YEARS.

THE BOMBING ALSO RESULTED IN OVER 1000 DEATHS (MOSTLY CIVILIAN) AND OVER 4 BILLION DOLLARS IN DAMAGE. ALSO, THE POLITICAL SITUATION IS NOW VERY PRECARIOUS WITH THE POTENTIAL FOR A RETURN TO SECTARIAN CONFLICT LOOMING.

OUTRO

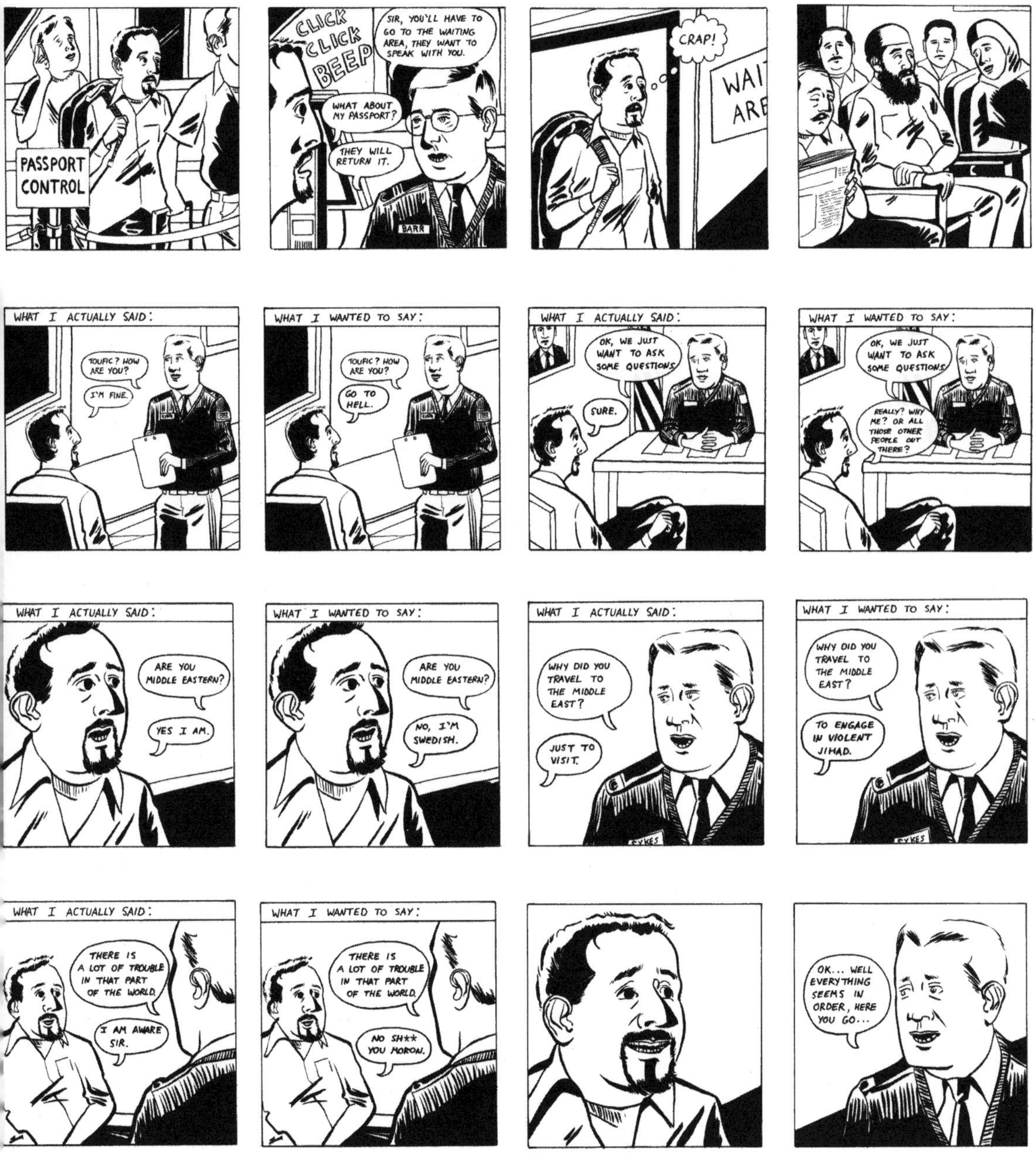
PASSPORT CONTROL
CLICK CLICK BEEP
SIR, YOU'LL HAVE TO GO TO THE WAITING AREA, THEY WANT TO SPEAK WITH YOU.
WHAT ABOUT MY PASSPORT?
THEY WILL RETURN IT.
BARR
CRAP!
WAIT ARE
WHAT I ACTUALLY SAID:
TOUFIC? HOW ARE YOU?
I'M FINE.
WHAT I WANTED TO SAY:
TOUFIC? HOW ARE YOU?
GO TO HELL.
WHAT I ACTUALLY SAID:
OK, WE JUST WANT TO ASK SOME QUESTIONS.
SURE.
WHAT I WANTED TO SAY:
OK, WE JUST WANT TO ASK SOME QUESTIONS.
REALLY? WHY ME? OR ALL THOSE OTHER PEOPLE OUT THERE?
WHAT I ACTUALLY SAID:
ARE YOU MIDDLE EASTERN?
YES I AM.
WHAT I WANTED TO SAY:
ARE YOU MIDDLE EASTERN?
NO, I'M SWEDISH.
WHAT I ACTUALLY SAID:
WHY DID YOU TRAVEL TO THE MIDDLE EAST?
JUST TO VISIT.
SYKES
WHAT I WANTED TO SAY:
WHY DID YOU TRAVEL TO THE MIDDLE EAST?
TO ENGAGE IN VIOLENT JIHAD.
SYKES
WHAT I ACTUALLY SAID:
THERE IS A LOT OF TROUBLE IN THAT PART OF THE WORLD.
I AM AWARE SIR.
WHAT I WANTED TO SAY:
THERE IS A LOT OF TROUBLE IN THAT PART OF THE WORLD.
NO SH** YOU MORON.
OK... WELL EVERYTHING SEEMS IN ORDER, HERE YOU GO...